MINDFULNESS MEDITATION
FOR BEGINNERS

Mindfulness
MEDITATION
for
BEGINNERS

50 Meditations to Practice
Awareness, Acceptance, and Peace

Dawn Mauricio

ROCKRIDGE
PRESS

Interior and Cover Designer: Mando Daniel
Art Producer: Janice Ackerman
Editor: Shannon Criss
Production Editor: Matthew Burnett
Illustration: © Marina Demidova/shutterstock.
Author Photograph: © Lisa Graves

ISBN: Print 978-1-646-11667-6 | eBook 978-1-64611-668-3

R0

This book is dedicated to the millions of Buddhist meditation practitioners who have come before me. Thank you for keeping this practice alive.

Contents

Introduction

You probably picked up this book because you're keen to start meditation. Perhaps your racing mind is causing you anxiety, preventing you from getting proper sleep, or causing you to be unkind and impatient, especially with those you love. Maybe, as was the case for me, you're turning to meditation as a lifeline to help you deal with overwhelming emotions. My name is Dawn Mauricio and I aim to provide you with a personal introduction to this practice. Like so many people, I came to mindfulness meditation because I was suffering. To be completely honest, though, at that time it felt very much like I came crawling to this practice.

In my mid-twenties, freshly out of an emotionally and verbally abusive relationship, I was having regular bouts of extreme anxiety. I would cry uncontrollably and often felt assaulted by my unrelenting thoughts. The only time I got a break from these emotions was when I practiced yoga. The physical sensations brought on by practicing yoga acted as a portal to mindfulness, and it was the mindfulness—being in the present moment—that brought me peace. Hours a day and days on end, I clung to my yoga practice like my life depended on it.

Soon after, I did what any well-meaning perfectionist would do: I started going on several silent meditation retreats each year and practicing for two to three hours a day. My mom and my partner at that time had a meeting with me that felt almost like an intervention—not because they thought I was joining a cult (although I'm sure that thought had crossed their minds), but because they both felt I was really impatient with them and got angry easily, despite my dedication to practice.

Of course, I thought *they* were the problem. However, what they said stuck. I soon realized that, by approaching meditation the way I did, I was using it as an escape from my problems and my role in them. This isn't the case for all serious practitioners, but it was certainly the case for me. I then committed to not attending a silent retreat until the desire came from wanting to connect deeply instead of wanting to escape. I also committed to reducing my daily practice time by more than half. Those two years of practice were incredibly challenging, as I was forcing myself to deal with the discomfort of daily life—like the ending of relationships, difficult work situations, or the news of the world—instead of fleeing.

The lessons learned during those two years have impacted my practice, my teachings—and me, on a personal level—more than I could have ever known. It is from that place that I teach and from there that what I share with you in this book originates. Almost two decades later, this practice has seen me through many highs and lows. The practice is not always pleasant, particularly when I'm feeling agitated, restless, or sleepy, or when I'm hit with a challenging time in my life and am filled with overwhelming emotions. Also, I tend toward anxiety, and so during anxious periods, getting to practice is challenging. But it is always worth it, and I'm still in awe of the ways this simple yet powerful practice provides me with a freedom I have yet to find anywhere else or in anything else. I have since completed various multi-year Buddhist and meditation programs, including several long retreats (one a three-month silent retreat!), as well as a four-year teacher training program. Thanks to my years of practice and teaching meditation retreats and mindfulness workshops, I have the opportunity to share mindfulness meditation with you.

As you make your way through this text, what I hope most is that you realize you don't need to go on a three-month retreat or embark on a four-year training program to start positively impacting your life and, by extension, the lives of those around you. All that is really needed is an open mind, a willingness to try something new, a sincere desire to see clearly, and a real yearning for more contentment and less suffering in your life and the lives of others.

With this practice, may you find steadiness, resilience, and joy.

HOW TO USE THIS BOOK

This book covers what you'll need as you begin your mindfulness meditation journey. In it, you'll find an introduction to mindfulness, 50 meditation practices you can do in various settings, and tips on how to continue with your practice beyond this book so that it becomes a mainstay in your life.

In part 1, you'll find a working definition of mindfulness, uncover the difference between mindfulness and meditation, get a brief background on the history of mindfulness, learn the essentials to practicing meditation, and become aware of other considerations as you set up for practice. Although it's not necessary to read part 1 in its entirety before you start meditating, I suggest you refer back to it regularly. Because your mind hasn't practiced being mindful for most of your life, it will most likely resist practicing at some point. Becoming familiar with the basic information in part 1 is helpful so that when you do feel resistance, you'll have the information and tools you need to validate your experience and overcome mental roadblocks.

In part 2, you'll find 50 meditations that range in length from 5 to 15 minutes. These meditations were designed to adapt to your practice on any given day, as well as to show you the broad scope of mindfulness. The meditations are suitable for all levels, and you don't need to work your way through them progressively. Ultimately, my intention—and hope—is that you'll try them all. The meditations can also be done more than once—in a day or in a life! They will grow increasingly accessible, but because we are constantly changing and evolving, they will remain novel.

Your journey doesn't have to end when your exploration of this book does. I'll share with you ways that you can continue to deepen your practice, as well as provide a list of resources that you can explore, at the end of this book.

PART 1
The Art of Mindfulness

It is likely that you've heard of the word *mindfulness*. In fact, you may have heard it so often that you know how to use it in a sentence in social settings—even though you don't actually know what it is!

Not to fret—this section of the book will lay it all out for you. You'll learn what mindfulness is and what it is not, different ways it can be practiced through meditation, tips and tricks to establish your own daily practice, and how to incorporate mindfulness into your daily life.

WHAT IS MINDFULNESS?

Mindfulness is a natural ability we all have, but we don't realize we have it because we are largely distracted or have never been taught how to recognize this quality. For example, when you're "in the zone" while playing a sport, making music or art, or intently watching a sunset, you are most likely being mindful without even knowing it.

Receptivity

Mindfulness is a quality of awareness that we bring to the present moment that is kind, curious, and nonjudgmental. It is seemingly simple, yet surprisingly difficult. Our task is to settle the mind and heart in such a way that we can be open to and observe life however it is occurring right now—that is, to be receptive to it—even if it means being with a busy mind or unpleasant emotion. This doesn't mean we should accept everything without question, though. With the information we receive, we then choose how we want to continue being mindful—remaining still or adjusting, with openness or resistance, for example.

Balance

Balance in mindfulness practice is not like balance in most other things. For example, when learning something new, like an instrument or language, a lot of persistence and patience are needed. At the beginning of our practice, mindfulness is no exception. Yet when we try to be mindful all the time, we get tired and burned out. We might think our practice isn't going well, and so we try harder, mostly because that works for a lot of the things in our life. But this can lead to more fatigue and more feelings of burnout, and it's at this point that a lot of people give up on mindfulness meditation.

In mindfulness practice, trying harder leads to an energetic imbalance, also known as *unwise effort*, which inhibits the sense of calm we're looking for. It's hard to know how much balance is needed—too little and we fall asleep, too much and we unknowingly block out the benefits. One of my teachers, Sayadaw U Tejaniya from Myanmar, would often instruct us to bring the same amount of effort to practice that it takes us to be aware of our 10 fingertips touching when we gently press them together. Try it and you'll see—mindfulness doesn't need much effort.

Nonjudgment

When we take something in through our senses—sight, smell, hearing, touch, and taste—an immediate classification happens. Based on our past experiences, whatever we sense gets categorized as good or bad, right or wrong, wanted or not wanted.

Nonjudgment, as part of the definition of mindfulness, doesn't ask us to stop this natural occurrence but to instead not be controlled by it.

Nonjudgment can also be described as acceptance, where the invitation is to accept whatever is arising with a spaciousness that neither grasps it nor pushes it away.

Patience

Mindfulness is a useful quality that acts as a guard to our reactions. It provides a pause, allowing us to take in what is happening. With practice, we start to discern ways to respond wisely.

What we might not realize, though, is that throughout this process, patience is being cultivated. For example, when we want this moment or this breath to be different somehow and we simply observe that desire without reacting, patience develops. This process is not to be underestimated. The more patience we can muster in our practice, the more we can bring it into our lives.

Awareness

Awareness is a nuanced quality that is used differently depending on the context or lineage of practice. To put it broadly, while mindfulness refers to our natural ability to be attentive in a given moment, awareness is a subtle quality that is a more spacious "knowing."

A simple analogy shows how the different concepts are related. Imagine you're a scientist looking through a microscope. Mindfulness is the microscope, the act of looking into it is meditation practice, being engrossed by the bacteria you're seeing is paying attention, and knowing you're at work in a lab and that you're looking down a microscope at bacteria is awareness.

When we practice, both mindfulness and awareness get cultivated. Therefore, I'll use these two terms interchangeably throughout the book.

MEDITATION

"Meditation" can mean many different things in different contexts, but here we use it specifically to mean the intentional practice of staying aware of the present moment. In other words, meditation consists of many techniques, most of which help cultivate mindfulness.

Typically, mindfulness meditation consists of anchoring your mind to a neutral "meditation object." This could be your breath, a physical sensation, or a sound, for example. The initial instruction is to place your attention on your meditation object, and whenever you notice that your mind has wandered, gently redirect your attention toward your object or point of focus.

The practice of meditation helps to develop concentration, and concentration acts as a doorway to cultivating mindfulness. In other words, meditation is a mind training of sorts, much like physical exercise is for the body. Just like you strengthen your muscles by going to the gym, you can begin to strengthen your concentration and awareness with a regular meditation practice.

Without concentration, mindfulness is still possible, although it is harder. This is because you probably spent decades letting your mind flutter from one thing to the next—like the past, the future, or some fantasy—and to suddenly want the mind to start resting on the present moment can feel impossible. As a result, cultivating mindfulness can feel challenging.

Paradoxically, in those difficult times, our task is to meet the moment where cultivating mindfulness can feel challenging with mindfulness. That is, we need to be friendly, kind, and patient with ourselves and how our practice is unfolding.

Why Does Meditation Work?

With mindfulness meditation increasing in popularity, there has been an explosion of studies to understand its effects. As reported in *Neuroreport* and *Psychiatry Research*, researchers found that after eight weeks of mindfulness practice, there were significant effects on the brain.

Four parts of the brain linked to healthy brain function saw significant positive changes: the left hippocampus, which is associated with learning and houses emotional regulators, such as self-awareness and empathy; the posterior cingulate, which is connected with wandering thoughts and self-relevance; the pons, where neurotransmitters that help regulate brain activity are produced; and the temporoparietal junction, which is associated with compassion and our sense of perspective. All of these parts grew in size, volume, density, or strength, resulting in all the qualities connected to these regions being nurtured.

Furthermore, the amygdala, the area of the brain that produces feelings of anxiety, stress, and fear, decreased in size. This change allows us to discern our emotional responses more clearly.

MEDITATION TYPES

The practice of meditation has a vast history, with roots tracing back to India, c. 5000 BCE. It also spans many traditions, from Christianity and Buddhism to Hinduism, Judaism, and Sufism. As a result, there are many ways one can practice meditation. The following is a list of the types of meditation that you will come across in this book; it is by no means an exhaustive list.

Concentration Meditation

Developing concentration is at the heart of most meditation techniques, yet certain practices focus particularly on this. Concentration meditation involves focusing on an object, a word or phrase, a sound, or a sensation and committing to sustaining that focus.

In my experience, being concentrated in meditation practice can feel pleasant. A sense of calm and a clear focus can arise, and for minutes at a time, the mind will easily and naturally block out nearby distractions. The catch is to not take this concentrated state to mean "This is what meditation practice should always be like." Just like life, your individual meditation practice will change, and when it does, it doesn't mean that you've done something wrong. It's simply what your practice is like right now.

Breath Awareness

Breath awareness meditation is a practice in which you anchor your attention on your breath. This can mean being aware of your breath at the nostrils, throat, chest, abdomen, in the back, or anywhere else you might feel it. For some, feeling the breath can seem abstract; in this case, employing a technique where you silently repeat "inhaling . . . exhaling" can serve as an alternative.

Breath awareness is one of the most popular types of meditation because we can be aware of our breath anytime and anywhere, keeping us tethered to this practice all day long.

Simply being aware of your breath may change it, but you don't need to intentionally control it. Breathing naturally is enough to ground the mind and connect you with your body. However, just because this is one of the most popular techniques doesn't mean you need to be able to practice it. For whatever reason—trauma or sickness, for example—being with the breath may be activating and not your means of practice at the moment. In this case, shift your attention to the body, sound, or sight instead.

Body Awareness

Body awareness is a type of meditation in which we become mindful of the sensations in our body. We can do this with a body scan, by feeling the sensations in a particular part of the body, or by noticing how experiences taken in through the senses manifest in the body.

Being mindful of the body helps us really get to know ourselves. The sensations present can let us know if a certain emotion is present, influencing our reactions. Being aware of our looks is not what this practice is about. Although there is a place for that in our lives, with this type of meditation we are trying to get to know ourselves from the inside out.

Movement Meditation

Movement meditation takes body and breath awareness and makes them more dynamic. This can be done by being aware of the body's sensations and the fluctuations of the breath while the body is in motion, or by integrating moments of pause throughout a given activity to check in with the body and breath.

Movement meditation can be quite freeing, bridging the techniques of a more still meditation into our daily life and granting us countless ways to practice throughout the day. As a result, we can awaken an entire panoply of experiences that we may have otherwise been asleep to.

Being mindful of your movements is not limited to any speed. What matters most is the quality of attention you bring to whatever it is you're doing.

Heart Practices

Originally taught as antidotes to fear and sorrow, heart practices focus on cultivating qualities such as loving-kindness, compassion, sympathetic joy, and equanimity. There are many ways in which we can engage in heart practices. The technique you'll find in this book uses the silent repetition of specific phrases, such as *May I be happy, May I be free.*

When engaged in the heart practices, it's totally normal to feel the opposite feelings of the quality you're trying to cultivate. Often, this type of meditation is a lot like cleaning a window that has been ignored for a long time. There might be a lot of grime on the surface, but eventually, with a sincere effort, the window becomes clear.

Visualization

Visualization entails using your imagination to bring images in your mind. We can visualize a certain experience with as much or as little detail as we like, although if we are new to this type of meditation, seeing detailed images may take some practice. Visualization meditation, in particular, involves focusing on an image or a person, like a loved one or yourself as a child. You'll come across both—visualization and visualization meditation—in this book.

Visualization isn't meant to be a promise but rather is meant to help you increase familiarity with a particular experience before you go through it, which can relieve any accompanying anxiety. It can also prepare you to react skillfully in a specific situation.

ORIGINS OF MINDFULNESS

The origins of mindfulness meditation can be traced back to Vipassanā or Insight Meditation, which is rooted in Theravada Buddhism. While Buddhism itself is a complex system of teachings and techniques, what you'll learn in this book are simply the techniques that are laid out in Vipassanā Meditation.

Buddhism, and by extension mindfulness meditation, was founded around 400 to 500 BCE in the eastern part of India by Siddhartha Gautama, who was later referred to as the Buddha.

Buddhism first came to North America in the 19th century via Chinese immigrants and steadily grew with the arrival of Japanese, Korean, and Taiwanese immigrants. They built temples and established strong practice communities. However, very few Westerners joined them, as their practices were seen as mysterious and unfamiliar.

Present-Day Mindfulness

Present-day mindfulness has been linked to American Buddhist meditation teachers Jack Kornfield, Joseph Goldstein, and Sharon Salzberg. Before becoming acquainted, they each traveled to South Asia in the late 1960s and early 1970s to learn and practice meditation. Unknowingly, they shared some of the same teachers, and after years of practice, their teachers authorized them to teach in the United States, encouraging them to create something together. They created practice communities that were separate from the existing Asian Buddhist communities, founding the Insight Meditation Society in 1975 and Spirit Rock Meditation Center in 1985, both of which now host tens of thousands of practitioners each year. Kornfield, Goldstein, and Salzberg have also each written numerous books, continue to participate in online courses and trainings, and are pillars in spreading the practice of convert Buddhism all over North America.

MYTHS AND TRUTHS ABOUT MEDITATION

One of the best ways to ensure that mindfulness meditation will become a regular part of your day is by debunking some false beliefs you have about it.

"I can't meditate because I have a busy mind."

This is the equivalent of thinking you're too dirty to shower! Mindfulness meditation helps calm the mind, yet some days you'll still have a busy mind. The goal isn't to stop thinking completely but instead to not get caught up in the content of your thoughts.

"I need to become a Buddhist before I can meditate."

You don't need to change your belief system or become a Buddhist to follow your breath or senses into the sensations of your body. These practices are universal and available to all.

"I don't want to practice because it'll turn me into a doormat."

Just as after being receptive in meditation practice you choose how to continue practicing, in life you take in what is going on around you and choose how to act. In my own experience, I have started standing up for what I believe in with a lot more confidence and clarity than before I started practicing.

"I don't have time to meditate."

You might not have time to meditate, but you certainly have time to be mindful. Because it is so all-encompassing, you can apply mindfulness to whatever you're doing. Try doing one or two tasks a day with a lot of mindfulness, like lathering your hair or body in the shower, brushing your teeth, or washing your hands.

"I need to have a special place and accessories before I practice."

Although having a special place to practice mindfulness would be nice, it's not necessary. You can practice while sitting in your favorite chair, standing in a park, or sitting up in bed.

"Mindfulness can only be done during meditation."

Since the quality of mindfulness is about the particular way we pay attention, it is not limited to the formal practice of meditation. In fact, when we can bring mindfulness into our daily lives, we'll be able to appreciate the scenery in front of us, the sounds around us, the food on our plate, and the emotions inside of us more fully.

"Mindfulness meditation is about being happy."

Mindfulness can help widen our perspective on life so much that we are able to be with the fluctuations of life without measuring our self-worth against them. This means being with the highs and lows, the pleasant and unpleasant, in a steady and resilient way. As a result, no feeling or experience gets left out. Wisdom gets cultivated with mindfulness, and with it comes the knowledge that even if we're unhappy in one moment, it will eventually pass.

"All I need to deal with my mental health is mindfulness meditation."

Mindfulness meditation can be an impactful and necessary part of your healing journey, but it is not meant to be the only tool in your toolbox. It cannot replace the wisdom, care, and guidance of a professional, nor can it regulate hormones or brain chemicals that a specially prescribed medication can. It is best to consult with your doctor or therapist to see if mindfulness meditation is appropriate for you at this time.

"Mindfulness is really just relaxation (and I do that all the time, so I don't need to meditate)."

Mindfulness and relaxation often get confused with one another, particularly because they complement each other well. When the mind races incessantly, anchoring it in the present moment can feel relaxing. As well, when the body is relaxed, mindfulness can arise more naturally. However, they are not the same. Mindfulness involves being aware of the moment regardless of what is happening, while relaxation focuses on releasing tension and anxiety.

"The goal of mindfulness meditation is to be mindful 100 percent of the time."

Not at all! Not only is it tiring, but being mindful 100 percent of the time would mean that you'd have to be in the present moment all the time. Sometimes, however, thinking ahead or about the past is useful. After all, especially as practitioners who don't plan to practice in a cave or monastery for extended periods, we need to make plans—and remember where we've left our keys! Instead of being mindful 100 percent of the time, the aim is to be mindful for short moments many times throughout the day.

THE BEGINNER'S MIND

Sometimes we think our practice should be a certain way, most often after we just had a pleasant meditation. However, if we don't catch ourselves, the next time we practice we may subtly try to recreate this past experience—and in doing so, drive ourselves crazy. That is the trap of "an expert's mind" or a mind "that knows."

On the other hand, whether your practice was pleasant or unpleasant, applying a beginner's mind can be refreshing and take the pressure off.

A good example of beginner's mind is a child playing in a new playground. They have a sense of curiosity, awe, and excitement as they play and explore their environment. They might squeal with excitement if something pleasantly surprises them or cry if they don't like something.

Applying beginner's mind to practice means approaching it as if it was the first time, when you were free of any preconceived ideas of what practice was supposed to be like. The idea of beginner's mind first came from the Zen Buddhist tradition. As Zen monk and teacher Shunryu Suzuki wrote in *Zen Mind, Beginner's Mind*, "In the beginner's mind there are many possibilities, in the expert's mind there are few."

CONTINUED

Of course, just because we decide to practice like this doesn't mean it happens easily. We need to constantly remind ourselves to be like a beginner. This constant coming back to the beginning represents the essence of any meditative practice, which is to allow there to be space to start over, and over, and over again.

UNDERSTANDING THE MIND

Occasionally people tell me they tried to meditate but couldn't "do it right." My response is to ask them to try to not be mindful for 15 seconds. That means to not hear any sounds, not feel, not see, not be aware of time as they try not to be mindful, and so on. Try it for yourself.

It's impossible, right? Even if you thought, "Hah! I wasn't mindful," you were actually mindful of not being mindful! All this is to say that we are always aware of something. The question then becomes, *Is what we are placing our attention on good for us? In what way is this helpful or unhelpful?* Apart from looking at the external things we pay attention to, like emails or the news, it's noteworthy to look at what we are attentive to internally, like our thoughts.

When we think negatively, processing thoughts and finding solutions becomes difficult because our brain coordination is slowed. For example, according to a study on the cerebellum and emotional experience published by *Neuropsychologia*, when we get scared from focusing on negative consequences, there is less activity in the cerebellum, which limits the brain's capacity to process new information. This in turn minimizes our ability to look for and identify creative solutions to our problem. Fear also affects the left temporal lobe, impacting our memory, impulse control, and mood.

In mindfulness practice, even though we are invited to be intentional and engaged with the moment by choosing what we focus on, we are not trying to do anything, be anything, or produce anything. Mindfulness practice meets us where we are.

If you're a person who thinks negatively, you might hope mindfulness is your way out. There is no doubt that it can be, but it doesn't happen from simply deciding you want to think positively. It happens when you soften and intend to meet your negative thoughts with a kind and present attention.

Mindfulness meditation isn't just about what is pleasant. It's about what is true, which contains both the unpleasant and pleasant, as well as the neutral. If you're thinking to yourself, "I picked up this book so I can be happy," you most certainly can be. By holding yourself and the paradoxes of life with kindness, especially in the times when you wish things were different, wisdom is cultivated, right along with happiness.

MINDFUL HEALTH

In recent decades, mindfulness has grown increasingly popular, leading to a rise in scientific studies about its impact on the mind and body. The results of a simple online search now reveal countless proven mental and physical benefits from practicing mindfulness.

Although mindfulness is incredibly powerful, it is not the only tool you'll need in your healing toolkit. I have found it most impactful when combined with other healing modalities, such as psychotherapy and trauma release work.

Stress

We have all felt stress at some point in our lives, whether it was before an exam, an unexpected expense, the sudden change in health of a loved one, or the demands of an unkind superior. Stress is our physical reaction to change, and even though some change can be positive—like getting a promotion in a new city or country, or having a new child—we most often associate stress with negative changes. Whether the change is positive, negative, good, bad, pleasant, or unpleasant, mindfulness *can* help reduce stress; an article in the magazine *Mindful* stated this in similar terms after reviewing studies from hundreds of universities. Some of the universities' suggestions for mindfulness included not taking your thoughts so literally; pausing before reacting; activating your "being" mode, which is linked to relaxation; and altering your attitude to change and to stress in general.

Anxiety

Anxiety is a little more complex than stress. Anxiety is often erroneously thought to be caused by the rumination of the mind, but it is actually the physical sensations that stem from the combination of a mental element like worry and a physical response like stress. For those who are familiar with the body's nervous system, anxiety emerges when the sympathetic nervous system (in charge of our fight, flight, or freeze response) or parasympathetic nervous system (responsible for rest and digestion) get triggered by mixed feelings or an inner conflict. The mind, in turn, interprets this inner conflict as a threat and triggers a fear response.

A study published in *JAMA Internal Medicine* found that a mindfulness program helped ease anxiety symptoms in people with generalized anxiety disorder. Whether your anxiety is an occasional occurrence or a common struggle, mindfulness can help with dropping the story and easing the worry. By noticing anxious thoughts, mindfulness encourages returning to the present moment.

Chronic Pain

The University of Minnesota found that when patients learned how to untangle their feelings or response to pain from the actual sensations of pain itself, they suffered less. This was done by using mindfulness meditation to become curious about the sensations of pain, not fighting them or trying to change them, while also using ways to manage attention if the pain ever got too intense. This is vastly different from painkillers that are designed to dull or get rid of pain.

Memory Loss

Memory loss occurs most often as we age because past memories inhibit our capacity to retain new and recent information, a phenomenon that researchers call *proactive interference*. A study published in the *Journal of Experimental Psychology, Learning, Memory and Cognition* found that participants experienced less proactive interference, showing an improvement in their short-term memory, with the help of mindfulness. Additionally, the better these participants performed memory tasks, the more their hippocampal volume increased; the hippocampus is the part of the brain responsible for the formation of new memories and associated with learning and emotions.

Addiction

A study conducted in Spain and published in *Frontiers in Psychiatry* applied mindfulness to a variety of addictions, ranging from substance use disorders to behavioral disorders. Researchers found that mindfulness-based interventions successfully reduced cravings and dependence, as well as improved emotional dysregulation and mood states.

In relation to addiction, mindfulness techniques help increase tolerance for discomfort and provide space and time to observe reactions, urges, and intended choices, as well as unveil the array of sensory experiences that already occur in everyday life.

Sleep

Although mindfulness and relaxation are often used interchangeably, they are complements to one another. For example, the act of slowing down and anchoring the mind can help you relax, while being relaxed can help mindfulness arise more naturally.

This is why mindfulness can help you sleep better. A study published in *JAMA Internal Medicine* found that anchoring a racing mind in a relaxed way with a mindfulness meditation technique helps ease any stress or anxiety in your system that may be getting in the way of a good night's sleep.

Problem Solving

If you've resigned yourself to believing that you're just not good at problem solving or coming up with creative solutions, mindfulness can help. In INSEAD's expert

opinion and management insights portal *Knowledge*,
Dr. Natalia Karelaia, associate professor of Decision
Sciences, reported that mindfulness amplifies creativity in large part by enhancing divergent thinking, a
process often used to bring about creative ideas by
exploring many potential solutions. An extra bonus for
experienced decision-makers is that mindfulness-based
techniques helped them detach from their ego, leading
to more openness and positively impacting the way
decisions are explored, made, executed, and evaluated.

Mood Disorders

Mindfulness has proved encouraging in the treatment
of mood disorders, such as depression, because it helps
people access a present-moment pathway. According to
Zindel Segal, a professor at the University of Toronto,
this is particularly significant when working with sad
mood states.

For example, patients who suffer from depression
repeatedly engage the mental pathways of narrative
self-reference and executive control, which weaken their
present-moment pathways. What's more, stress and
anxiety are serious triggers for depression. Meditation

can transform our relationship to these mental states, thereby delaying oncoming depression.

Blood Pressure

The benefits of mindfulness can also help with some physiological challenges, such as blood pressure. A 2019 study in the journal *PLOS One* found that mindfulness-based techniques, when used in a multimodal intervention that also consists of regular use of medications prescribed by participants' doctors, significantly reduced blood pressure levels. According to head researcher Eric Loucks, the study consisted of a 10-week mindfulness-based blood-pressure-reduction program that also included lectures on lifestyle behaviors that contribute to high blood pressure.

The results from the study were still in effect in participants' follow-up exams one year after the initial study.

GETTING STARTED

Each meditation in part 2 of this book gives general instructions on setting yourself up. In this section, you'll find more detailed information to prepare you for your mindfulness journey.

Practice Posture

When meditating, set yourself up as comfortably as possible. When your body is relaxed, it supports a relaxed mind. Unless otherwise specified, like in the walking or sweeping practices, your practice pose can be seated, standing, or lying down.

If you choose to sit, set your hips higher than your knees by sitting on a firm pillow or support. Find a spot on your seat that helps you keep your spine lengthened without much effort. This typically means you will be sitting towards the front of your support. Place your hands on your legs or in your lap with your palms facing up or down; you can close your eyes or turn them downward.

If you are injured, live with chronic pain, or have an illness, you may never find that "perfectly comfortable" position. Nonetheless, try to settle into a position that brings as much ease as possible.

Breath

At the start of every meditation, you'll be invited to take a few deep breaths. Not only is this a great way to intentionally start your practice because you are consciously separating whatever it was you were doing from your meditation, but it also is an intentional way to get the body and mind to relax. Although it may not happen every time, breathing deeply and taking a few sighs creates space in the body, mind, and heart. You don't need to be relaxed before meditating, but it does help. When a balance of relaxation and alertness is present, mindfulness can arise more naturally.

Mind

Generally speaking, mindfulness meditation can be broken down into four steps:

1. Pay attention to your breath (or another meditation object).

2. Notice when your attention has wandered.

3. Bring your attention back.

4. Repeat steps 2 and 3 a few billion times.

All this is to say, mindfulness isn't about being 100 percent mindful for the duration of your meditation. In Pali, the original language in which the teachings of Buddhism were written, the word for mindfulness is *sati*. Sati also means remembering, so in some ways, the practice of mindfulness is about remembering to be mindful as often as possible.

Self-Care

The practice of meditation is meant to be transformative, not traumatizing. Depending on your particular life history, some of the meditations may be triggering for no apparent reason. If things get overwhelming, please do not force yourself to endure the practice until the timer goes off. Instead, shift your attention to something else that feels neutral, perhaps also opening your eyes. Changing your attention is a wise action, and it does not mean you did something wrong nor that the practice is not for you. It just means that that particular way of meditating is not optimal for you right now.

RESET YOUR MIND

Getting discouraged with your practice will most likely happen at some point. I'm sorry if this is news to you, but I'm breaking it to you now so that when you *do* get discouraged, you can remember that it's completely normal to feel that way!

Feeling discouraged and unmotivated is bad enough, but these feelings can also lead to a pestering thought loop telling you that these feelings are contrary to what got you started on this path in the first place—which often leads to

CONTINUED

more feelings of frustration, making the whole experience all the worse.

When this happens, it's important to acknowledge the part of you that is yearning for some ease and wants things to go "right." That part of you simply cares about your well-being and might not have imagined the challenges along the way. If you react out of judgment, your meditation practice won't be a source of joy but rather another to-do item on a long list.

Whenever you've fallen off the wagon, so to speak, be gentle with yourself as you judge yourself and eventually recommit to practice. Keep things simple by starting with a length of time that feels really doable—not everything transformative needs to be hard! How long you practice and how many consecutive days you practice is not the be-all and end-all. What matters most is that you start again, no matter how many times you may have to.

BUILDING A DAILY PRACTICE

A little planning can go a long way. Before jumping right in with the meditations, think through some of the following details. They can contribute to a solid foundation for your practice.

Place

A practice space can be a designated part of your home that is as quiet as possible, is free from distractions, and has items that inspire a sense of ease, such as incense or a stone. A space such as this can be quite supportive; you don't have to set up or take down accessories, and any roommates or family members will know not to bother you when you're in this space.

However, not everyone has access to or can set up a designated space or has accessories such as these. This doesn't mean that practice can't be done. Mindfulness is about the quality of attention we bring wherever we are. You can meditate sitting up in bed or in a corner of your living room with a few items that inspire ease or practice.

Of course, mindfulness doesn't need to be practiced only at home! You can integrate it at work, walking outdoors, or even on public transportation.

Time

The practices in this book range from 5 to 15 minutes, and regardless of where you are in your mindfulness journey, you can start with any of them. Although you might believe the longer you meditate the better, that's not necessarily true. With mindfulness, quality matters more than quantity. If you choose to meditate for 15 minutes and it feels really hard, there's a chance you won't practice regularly. It's best to start with a short period of time and build up to a point where the practice feels challenging, but not unbearable.

Basically, there is no right length of time to practice. Instead, aim for a length of time that feels both spacious and slightly hard for you.

Consistency

There have been no conclusive findings on how long one should practice each day. The general consensus, though, is that practicing consistently yields the greatest benefits. In other words, it's better to practice 5 minutes every day than to meditate for 45 minutes once a week. Throwing yourself into practice once a week can feel disorienting and agitating, but practicing daily helps keep mindfulness accessible in your daily life. If something at work is testing your patience, you don't have to remember what it was like cultivating patience almost a week ago; instead, you just have to remember back to your last practice, either that morning or the night before. This helps bridge your meditation practice with your outer world, and seeing it come alive can motivate you to keep up with it on a daily basis.

Social Support

Although meditation practice, in a lot of ways, is done alone, practicing only on our own can feel isolating. When and where possible, practicing and discussing aspects of meditation with a group of people one or more times a week can really boost and energize your personal practice. Also, enlisting a friend with whom you share similar values and can have regular phone or text check-ins with can be uplifting. If these support options aren't possible for you, joining an online community where you can learn and explore what people are reflecting on can be motivating.

MINDFUL TERMS

Accept or allow: when asked to accept or allow an experience, you don't have to like it, just don't fight it

Agitated mind: sometimes referred to as "monkey mind," it's when your mind jumps from one thing to another, despite your best intentions

Anchor: what we place our attention on to ground us in the present moment; examples include the breath or a physical sensation

CONTINUED

Attention: a focused awareness that we apply when trying to cultivate the quality of mindfulness or when trying to be mindful

Buddhism: the practices in which mindfulness techniques are rooted; the Buddha was the first teacher of this tradition

Compassion: the natural response when a loving and kind heart comes into contact with suffering

Curious: an essential quality we bring to our mindfulness practice that combines kindness and interest to help us stay engaged

Embodiment: practicing mindfulness in a way where we are not thinking about practice but instead tuning in to how it feels in the body

Feeling tone: this natural, immediate, and often unconscious phenomenon of classifying experiences as pleasant, unpleasant, or neutral

Felt sense: being present with an experience from the "inside out" or from an embodied place, instead of an intellectual place

Heart: sometimes used interchangeably with *mind*; it can also mean your emotional or mental state

Heart quality: qualities of the heart, such as loving-kindness, compassion, or joy, which we already embody but tend to forget with our busy-ness

Insight Meditation: like an older relative of mindfulness meditation; it includes mindfulness techniques as well as the profound teachings of Buddhism

Intention: an aim, desire, or resolve that we set without being too attached to the outcome

Loving-kindness: a heart quality we all have that is friendly and benevolent; it can be uncovered with practice

May I: the recitation of heart practices starts this way so as to gently coax our natural state to rise to the surface

Meditation object: another way to say *anchor*, it is a present-moment experience we place our attention on

Mental noting: a method used when the mind is particularly agitated that consists of quietly naming what we are experiencing as we are experiencing it

Natural phenomenon: refers to experiences that are completely normal occurrences, whether they are sensations, mental states, or emotions

Neutral: in regard to feeling tone, neutral is shorthand for when an experience is neither pleasant nor unpleasant

Nonjudgment: an essential quality to meditation, it refers to being with an experience without trying to change it in any way

CONTINUED

Physical sensations: the bare physical feelings we experience, such as tingling, heat, or pulsations, before labeling them as something larger, like "pain"

Pleasant: experiences we tend to classify as "good" are really just pleasant, not tied to our self-worth

Present-moment experience: being with an experience right now, as it is, even if it's about something in the past or future

Sense doors: includes the five senses of seeing, hearing, smelling, tasting, and touching, as well as thinking as a sixth sense

Suffering: a broad word that includes subtleties such as discomfort, feeling "off," and being separated from what we want

Unpleasant: experiences we tend to classify as "bad" are simply unpleasant and don't mean we are bad or have done something wrong

Unwholesome: refers to actions or mental states that lead toward more suffering; can be used interchangeably with "unhelpful"

Wholesome: refers to actions or mental states that lead toward less suffering; can be used interchangeably with "helpful"

Wisdom: a quality of seeing things clearly that is cultivated with mindfulness practice

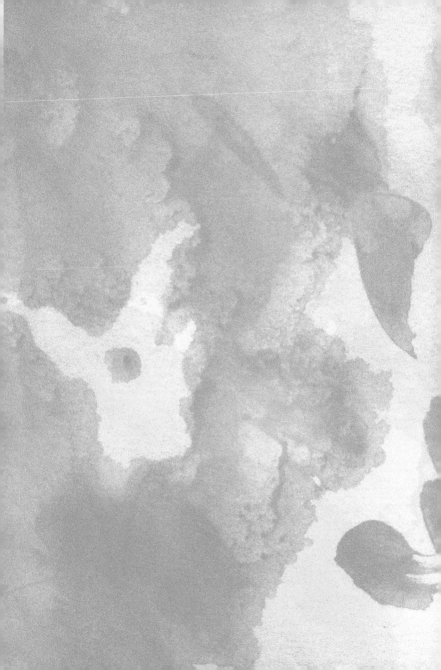

PART 2
Mindfulness Meditations

In this part, you'll find the heart and soul of the book. You can read all you want about the practice of meditation, but you won't access any of the benefits without practicing it.

There are 50 meditations provided here, ranging in length from 5 to 15 minutes. They are not arranged in any particular order, allowing you to adapt your practice on any given day. The meditations are suitable for all levels, and I hope you'll eventually try them all, exposing yourself to the broad scope of what this practice has to offer.

Stop and Simply Observe

Time: 5 minutes

> *"There are only two mistakes one can make*
> *along the road to truth: not going all the way,*
> *and not starting."*
>
> —*Unknown*

Some days it might feel utterly impossible to get to your designated meditation space for a formal practice. Not to fret! The good news is that meditation is a lot more accessible than we think. It's as simple as taking a moment to STOP—Stop, Take a breath, Observe, and Proceed. On those it's-impossible-to-meditate days, set your alarm to ring at some point during the day and block off 5 minutes for the following practice.

Steps:

1. Find a place to practice for a few minutes. It doesn't need to be anywhere fancy; you could lean against a wall, sit in your car or in front of your computer, lay next to a pile of laundry, or stand at a red light. If you're holding something, put it down or away so you can fully relax. If you feel comfortable doing so, you can also close your eyes.

2. Take a few slow, deep breaths. Either exhale deeply or let each breath go with a big sigh. Take as many of these breaths as you need. Whenever you're ready, return to your natural breathing, whether it's through your mouth or nose.

3. With your eyes open or closed, observe your surroundings—hear any sounds, sense any movements, see any objects, smell any smells, and feel any sensations that may be present in this moment.

4. After a few minutes of tuning in to your surroundings, blink your eyes a few times and proceed with your day.

Adjustment: This practice is easily portable and can be done in as little as 15 seconds! Just stop, take a deep breath, observe, and proceed.

Coming Home to Your Body

Time: 5 minutes

"Caring for myself is not self-indulgence, it is self-preservation, and that is an act of political warfare."
—Audre Lorde

Meditation is often mistaken as a mental practice, but really it is an embodiment practice. All the techniques aim to bring the body and mind into the same place—right here, right now. As easy as it sounds, it can be challenging because we are so used to running from one thing to the next, planning, strategizing, or worrying. Regardless of our best intentions, efforts, or resolutions, our mind will rest anywhere but "here." This practice, and mindfulness in general, helps us live in and through the body.

Steps:

1. After you've settled into your posture, whether it be sitting, standing, or lying down, bring your attention to your breath. For six slow, deep breaths, do your best to keep a relaxed, focused awareness on your breathing.

2. Expand this relaxed, focused awareness to include your entire body. You're not dropping your awareness of breath but widening your awareness to include both the breath and body. From head to toe, see if anything is attracting your attention. You're not looking for anything specific; you're just opening up your attention in a way that can receive whatever may be present. If nothing is attracting your attention, keep your awareness on your breath.

3. If or when a physical sensation is strong enough to become the dominant experience, place your awareness there, letting go of being with the breath for a few short moments. Use a simple word to describe what you're feeling, such as "tingling" or "heat." Afterward, return to being aware of your breath and body until another strong sensation arises.

4. Continue practicing in this way, going from the breath and the body to a physical sensation when one arises.

Rain on Your Emotions

Time: 15 minutes

"Emotions make us human.
Denying them makes us beasts."
—Victoria Klein

Sometimes we find ourselves reacting or having reacted to an experience almost as if we were possessed. When that happens, oftentimes it's because we were taken over by a strong emotion and didn't realize it. Alternatively, we may feel an intense wave of emotion coming on, which leads to our running away and avoiding it in such a way that it actually perpetuates harm or unhelpful patterns. Instead of spending our lives running away from or being ruled by our emotions, when we move toward them, we step out of the story and into the present moment, where we can access a different perspective and cultivate wisdom. This practice uses the acronym RAIN—Recognize, Allow, Interest, Nurture—to cultivate a new relationship with our emotions.

Steps:

1.   Listen and tune in to your own breathing while keeping a part of your awareness on your body.

2. Place one or both hands over your heart and check in. How are you in this moment? There is no right or wrong way to be. Lower your hands.

3. If a strong or intense feeling or emotion is present, can you name it? Without getting caught in any particular story or opinion, use one word to best describe it.

4. Can you allow and accept it being here? If what you're feeling is too subtle or too intense, simply place your attention back on your breath for the rest of the practice.

5. Be curious about all the ways you feel what you feel. Does your emotion manifest itself in your body as vibrations, pulses, pins and needles, throbbing? You may only notice the obvious sensations at first, and that's fine. With more practice, you will begin to become aware of subtler sensations.

6. Offer yourself a moment of nurturing. Some simple yet impactful ways to nurture yourself are silently repeating, "It's okay," or placing your hands over your heart and taking a few deep breaths.

CONTINUED

7. When the feeling no longer feels compelling, return to your breath until another feeling or emotion arises, at which point you can begin again.

Dawn of a New Day

Time: 7 minutes

"Every day is a new beginning.
Take a deep breath and start again."
—Unknown

We might have a general idea of how we want to be in our lives, but we don't often deliberately choose it in advance. This meditation uses visualization to help you integrate how you want to live in a way that is in line with your values. As a result, this practice is most effective if done at the start of your day, giving you agency over how you act and react, even if just for today.

Steps:

1. Place your hands on your torso to create a connection with your body. Relax into it.

2. After a few breaths, silently ask yourself, "What quality do I most want to engage today?" Focus on something you know you want to see more of, like patience, generosity, or kindness. You may already embody this quality to some degree; this practice is about manifesting it more regularly.

CONTINUED

3. When you know what quality you'd like to cultivate, set that intention by silently saying, "Today I am going to be . . ."

4. Think through what you have to do today—your morning, what you will do for lunch, who you will spend time with, the end of your day. Visualize this in as much detail as possible and imagine you're already living out the quality you want to manifest.

5. Identify what might be the most challenging part of your day. Loosely visualize how you would react to that situation while embodying the quality you intend to cultivate.

6. Finally, imagine yourself in bed at the end of the day, reflecting on the day's events. How would it feel to know you tried your best to live out that quality? You may not have been perfect, but you did your best.

Sink into Sleep

Time: 15 minutes

"Talk to yourself like you would to someone you love."
—*Brené Brown*

A lot of us live full and busy lives, starting the moment we wake up and ending the moment we go to bed. For many of us, though, our day doesn't actually end when we get into bed. If we didn't provide a spacious opportunity in the lead-up to bedtime to relax and unwind (without our devices), we might not realize we are still holding on—physically and mentally—when we lay down. This meditation invites you to really and fully settle into where you are with what you are trying to do—sleep.

Steps:

1. Snuggle yourself into bed and take a few deep breaths. Ground yourself in this moment by becoming aware of your body exactly as it is right now.

2. Laying on your back, get comfortable and commit to a relaxed stillness. Do your best to stay still, since movement activates the mind and brings energy to the body.

CONTINUED

3. Sink your body into the mattress. You may think you are already relaxed, but we unknowingly bring some of the holding on of our daily life into bed with us.

4. Place your hands to your body and take full, slow, deep breaths. With each exhale, tune in to your body, letting go and sinking into the mattress little by little. It may take time and be subtle. There's no rush.

5. At the same time, take full belly breaths that aren't forceful, as this, too, can increase energy. Breathe easefully, making the exhales a little longer than the inhales.

6. If your mind or energy is feeling some restlessness, scan your body from head to toe. Each time you scan over a part of the body, intentionally soften more deeply into the bed.

Challenge: Feeling pressured or stressed to sleep will only make it harder. When this happens, focus on paying attention to one half breath at a time.

Simply Standing

Time: 5 minutes

"Home, in the end, is of course not just the place where you sleep. It's the place where you stand."
—Pico Iyer

Standing is such a regular part of our lives that it is often taken for granted. If you have the fortunate capacity to stand, take a moment to be grateful for it, instead of realizing how precious it is only when your physical health is threatened.

We stand a lot more often than we think—for example, waiting for the bus, before we cross the street, or in line at a café. These in-between moments used to be a way to connect, but with technology, these times have become opportunities to jump into the information stream. This meditation turns a mundane moment into a possibility for a deeper connection.

Steps:

1. Stand with your legs coming straight down from your hips. Soften around the knees so that the weight of your body is being evenly distributed over the soles of your feet. Let your

CONTINUED

arms hang slightly away from the sides of your body and relax your shoulders and face.

2. Become aware of your surroundings—the temperature of the room, the lighting, sounds, and movements.

3. Feel your body. Without adjusting, notice if you're leaning more on one foot than the other, or more toward your heels than toes. After a few moments, gently sway back and forth and forward and back, trying to find a balance point.

4. Bring your attention to your feet, ankles, legs, hips, and lower back while simultaneously feeling your breath. Is the experience of your breath different while standing than in any other position? Note what feels true for you right now.

5. After a few minutes, once again become aware of your surroundings—the temperature of the room, the lighting, sounds, and movements.

Challenge: Standing still for any length of time can be hard on the feet, knees, or lower back. If you feel discomfort, mindfully make your way to a more comfortable position.

Listen In

Time: 7 minutes

"In every sound, the hidden silence sleeps."

—Dejan Stojanovic

If you have the ability to hear and haven't experienced any hearing issues, you may not have given your hearing much thought. But before it gets impaired, take a moment to celebrate it! Much like standing and walking, hearing happens all day long. We're just not usually aware of it unless something really pleasant—like birds singing—or unpleasant—like a jackhammer—catches our attention. This meditation will guide you through using sounds as an object of focus and show you that you don't need to react to everything you hear.

Steps:

1. Once you've settled into your meditation posture—sitting, standing, or lying down—tune in to the sounds and movements going on around you. There can even be an experience of hearing as a felt sense in the body.

CONTINUED

2. Observe sounds for what they are. Notice how they are constantly coming and going, outside of your control.

3. You don't need to do anything with the sounds—you don't need to add to them, change them, or make them go away.

4. Notice—without judgment, if possible—any changes in intensity and volume as sound continues to come and go.

5. Of course you will notice when sounds are pleasant and when they are not—this is part of mindfulness. If you find yourself getting tense in response to a sound, take a deep breath and relax. If you find yourself craving more of a sound, same thing, take a deep breath and relax. The sound will come and go, regardless of any holding on or pushing away you might do.

6. Tune in to the sensations in your body and notice any differences between when you resist a sound, grasp or want more of a sound, and when you simply hear a sound.

All the Feels

Time: 7 minutes

"May your choices reflect your hopes, not your fears."
—Nelson Mandela

There's a natural phenomenon that happens when you process stimuli through your senses—an unconscious categorization of the stimuli as pleasant, unpleasant, or neutral. In Buddhism, this is called feeling tone, or *vedāna*. It is worthy of exploration because our lives are chiefly spent strategizing how to increase pleasant feelings and avoid unpleasant ones. By regularly observing the feeling tone of an experience, we are cultivating a skill that helps us notice that things happening outside of us impact us on a subtle level, and from there we react. With practice, we can begin to see clearly and choose our reactions wisely.

Steps:

1. Begin the subtle practice of softening—relax your body, relax your effort. Meet this moment exactly as it is.

2. Turn your attention to your breath and feel it flow in and out naturally. Keep your awareness of your breath soft, relaxed.

CONTINUED

3. When a sound, feeling, or thought grabs your attention, notice if you have any subtle reaction to it. Do you like it, dislike it, or feel relatively neutral about it? Your relationship to the distraction gives you a hint as to whether you find it pleasant, unpleasant, or neutral. When the distraction is no longer gripping, return your attention to your breath.

4. The next time a distraction takes you away from your breath, tune in to your relationship with it. Once you've recognized the like, dislike, or neither liking or disliking of it, acknowledge that your reaction to it stems from a conditioned and uncontrollable response to regard it as pleasant, unpleasant, or neutral. You don't need to produce these feelings intentionally, since they arise on their own. You're just trying to notice them.

5. As the meditation comes to an end, commit to seeing how pleasant, unpleasant, and neutral experiences show up in your daily life and how feeling tone has an impact on the choices you make.

Tend to Your Talk

Time: 15 minutes

*"Honesty and openness is always the
foundation of insightful dialogue."*
—bell hooks

Speech can be an exciting area of practice, as well as vulnerable, revealing, and powerful. All forms of speech—spoken, written and inner—leave an imprint. Our words can break relationships, hide the truth, and divide communities, as well as unveil the truth and liberate. As a result, what we say matters, making this a valuable practice exploration. Try this meditation once or twice a day, starting with written speech and making your way up to phone interactions before in-person ones. Eventually, with regular practice, navigating even challenging conversations can feel more easeful.

Steps:

1. Before entering the space in which you'll speak—a meeting, social event, phone call, or text messaging conversation—clarify your intention. For example, I often have the intention to speak in a way that is kind, helpful, timely, and truthful—in alignment with my

CONTINUED

values. How do you want people to feel? Is there something specific you'd like to express? Acknowledge it and take a few deep breaths.

2. When you speak, keep part of your awareness on your body. This could be sensing your feet on the ground, your buttocks on the chair, or your hands wherever they're placed. One of my teachers, Sayadaw U Tejaniya, suggests trying to split your awareness 50/50—50 percent on your body and 50 percent on your speaking.

3. After you've spoken, tune in to how you're feeling. Sometimes, our energy gets the better of us despite our intentions, and we may have interrupted, gossiped, or spoken just to fill the silence. When listening, again split your attention 50/50 to include your body. If you're feeling uneasy or contracted, it might mean that your words or actions weren't in line with your intention.

4. As the conversation continues, see if you can align your words and actions even more with your intention. This might mean holding back on any urges to interrupt, fill the silence, or engage in divisive speech.

Adjustment: Try this first with a friend who is also curious about speaking mindfully. You can set up "dates" where you converse for 20 minutes a week, practicing speaking and listening mindfully.

The Journey Is the Destination

Time: 7 minutes

"Walk as if you are kissing the earth with your feet."
—Thich Nhat Hanh

Walking is something a lot of us get to do on a daily basis, whether we're walking to our car, from one place to another, or simply from our bedroom to the bathroom in the morning. During these times, however, we're often lost in planning the next thing we have to do, rehashing what just happened, fantasizing about something, or jumping into the information stream via our phones. The following meditation leads you through a formal practice of walking meditation.

Steps:

1. Find a pathway about 15 to 20 steps long, and begin to walk back and forth. We practice this going back and forth as a way to get out of the mind-set of "going somewhere"—this practice is a way to be here in the present while in motion. Keep your eyes gazing down a few feet

ahead of you, not looking at anything in particular. Choose a pace that gives you a sense of ease. Fast walking is helpful when you're agitated or sleepy. Slow walking is helpful when the mind is calm and alert.

2. When you come to the end of your path, stop, mindfully turn around, and start again. As you walk, let your attention settle into the body. Once you feel connected to your body, let your awareness settle into your feet and lower legs.

3. Feel the sensations of each step: your legs and feet tensing as you lift the leg, the movement of the leg as it moves through space, the contact of the foot with the ground, the cascade of sensations in the feet and ankles.

4. Whenever you notice that the mind has wandered, bring it back to the sensations of the feet and legs walking.

5. If an emotion or thought arises and grabs your attention, stop and be with it. As best you can, avoid getting caught up in story or judgment. When the emotion or thought weakens, return to your walking meditation.

Thought Clouds

Time: 10 minutes

*"A man is but the product of his thoughts.
What he thinks, he becomes."*
—*Mahatma Gandhi*

Some people come to meditation so they can quiet their minds but then stop meditating when they feel that their thoughts have become louder. With mindfulness, we're not trying to stop thinking, but rather we're trying to embrace the mind even when it's agitated and busy. Eventually, the mind may get more quiet and calm, but the real indication that your mindfulness of thoughts practice has progressed is in your ability to gently return your attention to the moment over and over again with kindness, no matter how many times it wanders.

Steps:

1. Start with a few deep breaths to help create space in your body, mind, and heart.

2. Place part of your attention on your buttocks touching your seat, your feet on the ground, or your body laying down. Place another part of your attention on your thoughts, watching them like clouds passing across the sky.

3. Whenever a thought is present, simply acknowledge that you're thinking by silently saying to yourself, "Thinking, thinking."

4. After some time, try to be more specific about what kinds of thoughts you're having—judging, planning, remembering, analyzing, or fantasizing, for example. If you get caught up with the content of a thought, that's totally normal. As soon as you notice that, bring your attention gently back to the parts of your body touching the ground. Remember, try to let your thoughts pass through your mind like clouds pass in the sky.

5. If your thoughts get overwhelming or you notice you've been lost in them for a while, take a deep breath or open your eyes briefly.

6. Bring your attention back to this moment, and when you're ready, close your eyes again. Continue observing your body and mind.

Challenge: If you unintentionally get caught in your thoughts and it brings up anxiety, open your eyes and look out a window or note the things you see until you feel more ease.

Connected

Time: 10 minutes

*"Learn the difference between connection
and attachment. Connection gives you power,
attachment sucks the life out of you."*
—*Unknown*

Given the broad capacity of mindfulness, we can begin to
unveil the unlikely ways in which we can be mindful outside
of the formal constraints of meditation. When we're able
to see this regularly, we start to understand that nothing is
outside the realm of mindfulness, including being mindful
with our phones.

Since smartphones have come into our lives, valuable
in-between moments that used to be opportunities to
connect have now become moments to jump back into
the information stream. The good news is we don't have to
completely give up our phones to find peace. Instead, we
can learn how to interact with them mindfully.

Steps:

1. It's best to do this meditation with your phone
   in hand. Go ahead and place it next to you
   before settling in to practice.

2. Take a few deep breaths, and then turn your attention to your body, feeling the parts that are touching the ground. Next, anchor your attention to the sensations of your hands—feel their position, temperature, pulsations, and whatever else you notice about them.

3. Stay connected to your body and open your eyes. Look around. If you feel like sight has pulled you out of feeling your body, practice moving your attention back and forth between your hands and whatever you may be looking at.

4. Reach for your phone, and as you do, feel your body moving. With the phone in your hand, feel its texture and temperature.

5. While holding your phone, return your attention to your body. Notice what your breath is like right now—if you unintentionally held or shortened it—and whatever else may be attracting your attention.

6. Feel if you have an urge to unlock your phone or open an app if you haven't already done so. Sense into how the urge feels—contraction or

CONTINUED

expansion, for example. Feel free to interact with your phone while moving your attention back and forth between what you're looking at and your body.

7. Take a deep breath. Put your phone down and place your hands on your legs or by your sides. Lift your head, lengthen your spine, and once again reconnect with the parts of your body touching the ground.

Adjustment: Try this in front of your computer, feeling the keyboard beneath your fingers and tuning in to how what is on the screen is impacting you.

Befriending Yourself

Time: 7 minutes

"You are your best thing."
—Toni Morrison

Some days, the thought of becoming our own friend can feel impossible, while other days it can feel selfish. In both cases, we'll bypass befriending ourselves, and instead, we'll quickly be loving and kind to others. But it's imperative that we start with ourselves. Much like how we are told in an airplane to secure our own oxygen mask before helping others in the case of an emergency, we won't be able to love and accept others in a profound way if we don't love and accept ourselves first.

Steps:

1. Begin in a position that expresses the loving-kindness you have or wish to have. Let your body relax and be at rest. Quiet the mind by focusing on the sensations in your body or on your breath for a couple minutes.

2. Picture a younger version of yourself when you may have needed some loving-kindness

CONTINUED

but didn't get it. It could be you as a child, a teen, or an adult, even as recently as today.

3. Silently recite the following phrases, directing them to this younger version of yourself. Leave a pause between the phrases so the words can really sink in.

May I be happy and healthy.
May I be free from inner and outer danger.
May I be held with compassion.
May I love and accept myself just as I am.

4. Let any feelings arise with the words, even if they seem contradictory to this practice. If need be, adjust the words and images so that you find the exact phrases that best open you.

5. After repeating the phrases over and over for a few minutes, come back to your breath or body. Notice any feelings and emotions that have arisen, without trying to change them.

Challenge: It's completely normal for the exact opposite feelings, like anger or judgment to arise with this practice. Be gentle with yourself when these types of feelings arise.

Rock It

Time: 5 minutes

*"When I let go of what I am,
I become what I might be."*
—Lao Tzu

I love this practice because it is jam-packed despite its simplicity and length. It uses the acronym ROCK as its foundation: Relax, Observe, Curiosity, Kindness. Relaxation is key to this kind of meditation, because it helps mindfulness arise more naturally and effortlessly. From there, we are able to tune in to our surroundings without getting caught up in them, establishing a place for curiosity and kindness to arise with our intention to relax, whether we like what's going on or not. All this makes for a perfect recipe for developing wisdom.

Steps:

1. After you've settled into your meditation position, take a few deep breaths. Let them out with either big exhales or audible sighs. Do this as many times as you like, eventually returning to breathing naturally.

CONTINUED

2. Relax the parts of your body that don't need to be holding on right now. You can do this by either scanning your body from head to toe or silently saying to yourself, "May I relax" or "May this body relax." It's very possible that you'll need to remind your body to relax more than once during this meditation and that's not a problem! Relaxation is an open invitation.

3. Tune in to your surroundings, noticing anything that is attracting your attention. All distractions are welcome—physical sensations, sounds, or thoughts. Whatever you're noticing, try to be curious about it as much as possible. The difference between being distracted and noticing distractions is that, with the latter, mindfulness is your companion.

4. You might get pulled into particular thoughts, such as "That sound shouldn't be happening," or "Don't they know I'm meditating?!" As soon as you notice, be kind to yourself, perhaps even playfully laughing at your mind.

Adjustment: This practice is versatile! Try it as a practice on its own, right before another practice, or any time during the day.

Get Down with This

"Some of us think holding on makes us strong;
but sometimes it is letting go."
—Hermann Hesse

A common obstacle to people starting and maintaining a meditation practice is that they think they have to practice sitting in a certain way. With all the photos of people looking peaceful in complicated seated positions, it's easy for tight-hipped folks to think we're just not made for meditation. Au contraire, meditators! The Buddha taught that we can practice in any position—standing, sitting, walking, and lying down. This practice explores the ways in which you can be mindful in a comfortable, reclined position.

Steps:

1. As you set yourself up, make sure your head is slightly propped and that you are laying on your back on a soft surface. If possible, have this be a different place from where you would normally sleep or nap, as a way to let the body know you are doing something new in a familiar position.

2. If you are feeling sleepy, bend your arms and place your elbows by your sides in what I call the "robot arms" position. In this position, your fingers will be pointing up to the ceiling.

3. Take a few deep breaths. With each exhale, now and for the duration of the practice, see if you can let your body sink deeper into the surface you're on.

4. Feel the parts of the body touching down, such as your heels, calves, buttocks, hands, parts of your back, and your head.

5. Tune in to the parts of the body that are not touching the ground, like the backs of the ankles, the backs of the knees, the lower back, the backs of your wrists, and the back of the neck.

6. Feel your entire body all at once, being particularly mindful of any sensations that are attracting your attention.

Challenge: When meditating reclined, you may get sleepy. This often means that your body hasn't yet recognized this as a practice position. Keep at it! Your body will eventually get it.

Take Note

Time: 5 minutes

"Every breath we take, every step we make, can be filled with peace, joy, and serenity."
—Thich Nhat Hanh

People often assume that if they have a busy mind they can't meditate. But it's exactly for that reason why we should try to learn to meditate! Some days, the mind can feel busier than other days, and the temptation to skip our meditation practice on those days can be strong. Instead of skipping it, give the busy mind what it wants—something to do! This practice of "mental noting" is great for anxious, impatient, and even sleepy practice days.

Steps:

1. To help you settle, take a few deep, full breaths and let them go with big sighs. Eventually, find a breath that feels easeful.

2. Tune in to the qualities of your breath. What is it like right now? Try to keep a spacious and relaxed awareness of your breath. If it's helpful, place one or both hands on your chest

or abdomen to physically feel the rise and fall of the breath at this place.

3. Begin to mentally note your direct experience. When you inhale, silently say, "Inhaling," and when you exhale, silently say, "Exhaling." Make sure to keep the "internal volume" of your mental noting low so you can continue to refine your awareness of how the breath feels.

4. As your attention drifts, gently return to your breathing.

5. Before the end of the practice, let the mental notes go and simply relax for a few moments. Just be, noticing how you are feeling now.

Love Yourself

Time: 10 minutes

"Kindness is more important than wisdom, and the recognition of this is the beginning of wisdom."
—*Theodore Isaac Rubin*

Loving-kindness or friendliness is a quality in mindfulness meditation that can significantly transform how we relate to ourselves and others. But just because we decide we want to be loving and kind doesn't mean we become so immediately. The good news is that loving-kindness is a quality that can be cultivated. At first, the opposite feelings of loving-kindness may arise, but eventually, we begin to love ourselves wholly and fully, including really and truly loving our faults. Once we do that for ourselves, we grow to love and accept those around us wholly and fully, too.

Steps:

1. Begin in a position that expresses the loving-kindness you have, or wish to have. Gently gather your attention around the sensations in your body or on your breath.

2. Bring to mind the different parts of yourself—the everyday version of yourself you see in the mirror, the lovable part, the wise and intuitive

teacher, and the mysterious parts. Take a moment to acknowledge and thank them all for coming together to make up the unique expression of life that is you.

3. Sense into which part of yourself needs some loving-kindness today. Let the other parts stand to the side as you begin to offer loving-kindness phrases to that part of you.

May I have physical well-being.
May I be free from danger.
May I be kind to myself.
May I dwell in peace.

4. Let any feelings arise with the words, even if they seem contradictory to this practice at first.

5. Repeat the phrases over and over.

6. Eventually, come back to your breath or body after reciting your last phrase. Notice the feelings and emotions that have arisen without judging them or trying to change them.

Adjustment: When time allows, send loving-kindness to all the parts of yourself, one by one, and then ending with all of them together.

Feel It, Heal It

Time: 10 minutes

"Nothing can dim the light which shines from within."

—*Maya Angelou*

No matter how much we might try, we can't control the things that happen around us, or to us. We can, however, learn how to act, or react, skillfully. Doing so takes an awareness of our emotions. A lot of us, however, grew up in ways where being aware of our emotions wasn't taught or encouraged. Like so much of mindfulness, it's a skill that can be cultivated. We start by paying attention to our emotions in practice and eventually in our day-to-day lives. This helps us to not be ruled by them and leads us to choose wisely based on what we're feeling.

Steps:

1. Whatever position you've chosen for this practice, be sure you're able to breathe with ease.

2. Tune in to your breathing while also checking in with yourself. How are you arriving to this moment? You may be feeling tired or joyful,

inspired or grieving, energized or confused, sleepy or excited, anxious or peaceful. As best you can, name your particular experience.

3. It's very possible you don't like what you're currently feeling. See if you can relax around it by taking a few deep breaths.

4. When you're ready, get really curious about what you're feeling. Does it—the excitement, sleepiness, anxiousness, happiness, or whatever your experience may be—manifest in your body as vibrations, pulses, pins and needles, throbbing? Does it feel dynamic or like a block? Light or heavy?

5. When there's nothing left to explore in regard to your feeling, return to your breath until another feeling or emotion is strong enough to take your attention away from your breath. If or when that happens, begin this exploration again.

Good Grief

Time: 10 minutes

"Often when you think you're at the end of something, you're at the beginning of something else."
—Fred Rogers

Grief can be an extremely unpleasant emotion, but it's not inherently bad, and if we're feeling it, it doesn't mean we've done something wrong. All emotions have a role in our lives and grief helps us process loss. This practice helps us welcome the waves of grief with tenderness, so that grief can move through our system and create space for growth and resilience.

Steps:

1. Create an atmosphere of support, practicing amidst things that bring you care and comfort—a fuzzy blanket, a warm sweater, or soft pillows, for example.

2. Feel your breath in your abdominal area. Create connection and warmth by resting one hand on your abdomen and the other on your heart, holding yourself gently.

3. Keeping part of your attention on your breath and hands resting on your body, bring to mind your grieving and your sadness. Allow for any images, feelings, and parts of the story to arise on their own. When they do present themselves, hold them and the part of yourself that is grieving with tenderness.

4. If the practice ever gets too intense, shift your awareness from your grief and rest in something that is more neutral, for instance, by opening your eyes and looking out the window. By doing so, you're enabling your system to be able to handle the next wave of sadness.

5. Whatever you're feeling is completely natural. There's no need to make what you're feeling the enemy, even if it's very unpleasant. It is simply the loss moving through your system, clearing space for something else to eventually grow.

Challenge: Sometimes grief can feel so intense that easing off is a wise choice. Go for a walk, watch something light, talk to a friend. Eventually, return to tending to your grief.

Lean Back

Time: 10 minutes

"I'm not going to say it wasn't hard. But I had to let go. And I learned that when you not only let go, but open your arms wide and learn the lessons, that an experience—no matter how bad—can teach you. That's when you rise."

—Ann Curry

In a world where it's not just commonplace but expected of us to always be thinking ahead, our body tends to follow suit. Without our realizing it, we typically lean forward when walking and sitting, a reflection of our minds being "one step" ahead of our bodies. It then becomes a chain reaction: the future-oriented mind incites the body to lean forward, leading to the mind trying to keep up, and so on. By being attentive of our back body, we can begin to settle back into this moment, right where we are.

Steps:

1. Settle into a relaxed pose and take a few deep breaths to help you arrive.

2. Feel your body's position and lean slightly back, stacking your head over your heart over

your hips if you're seated or standing. If you're lying down, sink your entire back body into the ground.

3. Bring your attention to the top of your head, the back of your head, and the back of your neck. Notice any sensations you may feel in these areas. As you scan over these parts, see if you can physically or energetically lean back into them a little more.

4. Tune in to your arms, your shoulders, the back of your upper arms and forearms, your wrists, and the tops of your hands. Are any sensations attracting your attention?

5. Tune in to your back and do the same thing, sensing into the upper, middle, and lower back. What sensations are present?

6. Next, tune in to your buttocks, back of your thighs and knees, and your heels. What do you feel in these areas? You're not looking for anything in particular; you're simply being open to whatever might be there.

CONTINUED

7. Finish this back body scan by being aware of your entire back body all at once.

Adjustment: Try this practice of leaning back into your back body when eating and notice if it changes the quality of your attention while eating, or even how fast or slow you eat.

Share the Goodness

Time: 12 minutes

"Love is an action, never simply a feeling."
—bell hooks

It's easy to think that one of the goals in meditation is to be loving and kind, all the time and to everyone. But as anyone who has tried that knows, it's not really possible and trying is pretty exhausting. We don't need to love everyone— simply tolerating some people can feel like enough work! So instead of measuring yourself against how you think you should be, celebrate how far you are from hate, the opposite of loving-kindness, because although seemingly insignificant, it's a movement in the right direction.

Steps:

1. Set yourself up in a caring and comfortable position. Settle your mind by tuning in to your body or breath.

2. When you feel ready, extend your wishes of loving-kindness to others. Start with a benefactor, someone who has taken care of you. If it's easier, you can even send loving-kindness

CONTINUED

to a child or an animal. Picture them and recite your loving-kindness phrases a couple times.

May you be happy and joyful.
May you be safe from inner and outer harm.
May you be well in body and mind.
May you be peaceful and at ease.

3. Finish this round by coming back to your breath or body after reciting your last phrase. Notice what feelings and emotions are present now.

4. Next, expand this practice to a neutral person, someone you may see somewhat regularly but don't really have positive or negative feelings for.

5. If you feel ready, expand your focus to include others: friends, neighbors, even people who you find difficult.

6. Finally, end the practice by sharing the loving-kindness with all beings, near and far.

Challenge: This practice can be done on its own or along with sending loving-kindness to yourself for a more complete practice.

Dig Doing the Dishes

Time: 15 minutes

> *"Work is love made visible."*
> *—Kahlil Gibran*

I mostly love washing the dishes because I find that there is something soothing and meditative about it. But I don't always feel like that, especially when I'm tired or when a big pile is waiting for me. In those cases, approaching the task like a practice makes it a lot less intimidating. I can stay focused on the very dish or utensil I'm cleaning instead of resenting how much I have left. Whether you initially love doing the dishes or not, being with one dish at a time helps us get in touch with the simple pleasures that are present in everyday chores.

Steps:

1. Stand in front of your sink and take a few deep breaths to create space in your body and mind.

2. Look at the dishes you have to wash and notice if any reactions arise along with the sense of seeing.

3. As you turn on the water, be present for the process of getting the "right" temperature.

CONTINUED

Catch the mind as it goes from unpleasant when the water is too hot or too cold to pleasant.

4. Feel the sponge's texture as you add soap to it, and watch the dab of soap dissolve into the sponge as you wet it. Turn off the water.

5. Pay attention to what you want to start with. Utensils? Glasses? Plates? Bowls? Notice this intention and then proceed. As you wash, feel your hands and arms, the texture of the soap and sponge, and any noises going on around you.

6. When it comes time to rinse, again be mindful as you get the right water temperature. Watch the soap and food residue rinse off the dishes into the sink.

7. Feel your body move as you place your dish in the drying rack or dishwasher.

8. Repeat until all your dishes are done, which might feel sooner than you think.

Bless Your Stress

Time: 12 minutes

"You may not control all the events that happen to you, but you can decide not to be reduced by them."
—*Maya Angelou*

Stress can feel very real and has real effects on our health. Stress arises when we feel that the demands on us exceed what we're able to handle. In other words, stress comes from the thoughts we create from feeling pressured by outside sources. We might think the way to relieve stress is to check off to-do items on our list, but that is a fleeting reprieve from the feeling. Instead, freedom lies in feeling the stress. It may sound paradoxical, but doing so gets us out of our stress story and into the moment.

Steps:

1. Settle into as comfortable a position as possible. We tend to hold the body when we're stressed, and being comfortable will help invite the body to relax.

2. Take three to six consciously deep breaths. If you're in a space that allows for it, let each

CONTINUED

deep breath go with an audible sigh. The more stressed you're feeling, the louder the sigh.

3. Tune in to your body. Notice any palpable sensations from having taken those deep breaths. Also notice if there are any tense areas in your body that can be coaxed into releasing, like your eyebrows or eyes, jaw, shoulders, abdomen, or hands.

4. Get curious about the remaining sensations related to your stress. Feel any shortness of breath, contraction in the body, tingling, lightness of energy, or whatever else you can sense into. As best you can, bring yourself back from thinking about the stress to once again feeling it.

5. Notice if the sensations get stronger, weaker, disappear, or stay the same. We're not trying to change what's happening or create a particular experience; rather, we're trying to cultivate a steady resilience, regardless of our external circumstances.

Lend a Hand

Time: 7 minutes

*"It is in your hands to create a better
world for all who live in it."*
—Nelson Mandela

The Buddha taught that enlightenment can be attained in any meditation posture—sitting, walking, standing, or lying down. On top of that, integrating mindfulness with movement, like in walking meditation, increases our chances that we'll be mindful more times during the day. But some days, though we might feel the need to combine mindfulness with walking, we might be too tired or unable to walk due to illness, injury, or pain. In that case, we can use our hands and arms to ground our awareness practice in our bodies.

Steps:

1. If you're seated, place your hands on your thighs, palms facing down. If you're lying down or standing, place your hands and arms by your sides, palms down if you're lying down and in whatever way is comfortable if you're standing.

CONTINUED

2. Tune in to this moment, particularly noticing if there are any sensations attracting your attention right now.

3. Gather your awareness onto your right hand and feel whatever sensations may be present there—tingling vibrations, pulsations, warmth.

4. Begin to slowly turn your right palm to face the ceiling or sky, paying attention to all the micro-movements and sensations the hand goes through to complete this action.

5. Lift your right arm toward the sky or ceiling. Any amount of lift is perfect. There is no need to force beyond what feels good. Again, apply curiosity to this entire movement.

6. Turn your palm to face the ground, and slowly lower your arm and hand back to your starting position, being really aware of anything that arises.

7. Once your hand touches down, tune in to any sensations present in your whole body, and sense any differences between your right and left side.

8. Repeat this process with your left hand and arm.

Meeting the Judge With Kindness

Time: 10 minutes

"I think every single imperfection adds to your beauty. I'd rather be imperfect than perfect."
—Sonam Kapoor

The judging mind is strong and our relationship to it is complicated. It can be a source of an unhealthy motivation as well as shame; in both cases, the harm caused by judging ourselves is longer lasting than any "good" that comes from it. The judging mind tends to scrutinize who we are instead of what we did. Although we might not always act wisely, our ability to recognize that in those moments the wounded part of ourselves got activated and reacted will reduce any shame or judging cycles we may get caught in, establishing a ground for our resilience.

Steps:

1. Begin in a position that expresses the loving-kindness you have or wish to have. Invite your body to relax by taking a few deep breaths or silently saying to yourself, "May I relax."

2. For a few minutes, settle the heart and mind further by paying attention to the sounds around you, the sensations in your body, or your breath.

3. Bring to mind your fragile and wounded part. This is the part of you that sometimes gets activated, and in those times, doesn't make the wisest decisions, really just out of self-preservation. Offer loving-kindness to this version of yourself.

    May I be peaceful.
    May I know safety and the causes of safety.
    May I be kind to myself.
    May I accept myself as I am.

4. Let any feelings arise with the words, holding them and yourself with kindness.

5. Repeat the phrases over and over.

6. Eventually come back to your breath, body, or sounds after reciting your last phrase. Notice the feelings and emotions that have arisen without judging or trying to change them.

Mindfully Consuming Media

Time: 15 minutes

> **"Emotions are not a choice. Behavior is."**
> —*Mark Manson*

Listening to music or podcasts, watching binge-worthy series, and reading the news have been part of our lives for a while now, but in recent years, these activities have started swallowing up large parts of our awareness. What we might not realize is that what we take in via our eyes and ears has an impact on our bodies, much like the food we eat or the products we use—that's why the term "consuming" is used here. But similar to food, when we start bringing mindfulness to the media we consume, we can choose between the ones that create stress and anxiety and the ones that bring wisdom, knowledge, connection, and growth, as well as how we take them in.

Steps:

1. Before jumping into consuming your chosen media, take a few deep breaths.

2. Tune in to your body. What sensations are present? Would you classify them as pleasant, unpleasant, or neutral?

3. Press play on your movie or music or start reading your article. After a couple of minutes, pause watching, listening, or reading and check in with your body again. What is here? Can you name the feeling or sensations? Repeat this step a few times.

4. Once you've built up your awareness with your chosen media, try splitting your attention 50/50 while you're engaged in the watching, listening, or reading. This means being partly aware of your body while also watching, listening, or reading. After a few minutes, press pause again and reflect on how much you were able to be aware of your body during that last round. There is no right or wrong; you are simply doing your best to cultivate this new skill.

5. Before proceeding, once again check in with your body. What feelings or sensations are present? Are they pleasant, unpleasant, or neutral? Tuning in to these feelings will eventually influence the types of media you engage in and how often.

Countdown to Ease

Time: 5 minutes

*"Now that I knew fear, I also knew
it was not permanent. As powerful as it was,
its grip on me would loosen. It would pass."*
—Louise Erdrich

Anxiety can come on subtly as agitation, nervousness, and tension, or it can come on suddenly as panic and dread. In either case, anxiety can lock us into a sort of tunnel vision, which then starts a chain reaction—the limited perspective sparks more anxiety which limits our perspective further, leading to more anxiety. In the moments when we have a sliver of mindfulness, we can try the following countdown. It is an immediate way to get out of our heads and into the present moment, creating a bigger container, or widening our perspective in a way that helps ease our anxiety.

Steps:

1. Ground yourself in this moment by taking a few deep breaths or feeling your feet on the ground.

2. Keeping your eyes open, take a moment to acknowledge five things you can see, pausing

before moving on to each sight. Ensure taking them in by saying the name of each thing out loud or silently to yourself.

3. Feel four sensations in your body. Again, really take them in by saying them out loud or silently to yourself. Pause before moving on to the next sensation.

4. Notice three things you can hear. Shift your attention so you can take in three different sounds, instead of noting the most dominant sound more than once.

5. Become aware of two things you can smell. If nothing seems apparent to you, try smelling your clothes, or feel free to move to a place where odors may be stronger.

6. End this practice by finding one thing you can taste. You might tune in to the last thing you drank or ate. If that's not accessible, bring to mind your last meal and any tastes that were present then.

Adjustment: If you are prone to anxiety, practice this meditation regularly when you're not anxious so that it can become increasingly accessible in those anxious times.

Sweep Your Body for Sensations

Time: 5 minutes

"The past, the present and the future are really one: they are today."
—Harriet Beecher Stowe

Sweeping your body and tuning in to its sensations is an effective tool to quickly drop into the present moment. First, the body is with us wherever we go—we just often forget it's there because we spend so much time up in our heads. Second, feeling the body's physical sensations actually helps ease stress and pain, increase our tolerance for discomfort, and improve relaxation; it can eventually get us to be more connected to our emotions and feelings, leading us to act more skillfully. As a result, this is an incredibly impactful and promising practice, despite its simplicity.

Steps:

1. Settle into a relaxing position and take a few deep breaths to help you arrive.

2. Bring your attention to your head and face and feel whatever you feel in these areas. Tune in to the top of your head, forehead, eyes, cheeks,

jaw, mouth, and chin. Relax any of these parts if they are tense or if you're holding on.

3. Do the same thing with your neck and torso. What is attracting your attention in the front and back of your torso? What sensations are present? Perhaps it's spaciousness, tingling, or tension. You're not looking for anything in particular—you're simply being open to whatever might be there.

4. Become aware of your lower body—your pelvis, legs, and feet. What do you feel in these areas? There's no right or wrong answer; there is simply your experience as it is right now.

5. It's quite possible that in some parts of your body you notice more the absence of sensation. That's completely fine—you haven't done anything wrong.

6. Feel your entire body all at once—the parts touching the ground, any sensations present, even feel the space around your body.

Just This One Breath

Time: 5 minutes

"Joy and life exist nowhere but the present."
—*Maxine Hong Kingston*

Paying attention to the breath is often the first instruction given to beginners, yet it can be an effective way of practicing no matter what your level of experience. The reason why the breath is one of the most common meditation anchors is that it is always with us, wherever we go. As a result, no matter where we are, tuning in to the breath, even if for just one breath—something relatively simple—can shift our perspective in profound ways.

Steps:

1. Bring a relaxed awareness to your breath. Take a few easy, deep breaths and release them.

2. Without changing or controlling your breath, notice what it is like right now. For example, is your breath deep, shallow, smooth, choppy, easeful, or strenuous? Despite any opinions you may have about how you "should" be breathing, there is no right or wrong way to

breathe. There is just your breath, as it is, right now.

3. It's possible that it's hard to tune in to your breath because it's so subtle. Relax any effort and be aware of anything you do notice regarding your breath. For example, where do you feel the breath the most in your body? Do you feel it most moving in and out of your nostrils or in the expansion and contraction of the chest or abdomen? Wherever you feel it most, place your attention there. If it helps, you can place your hand on your chest or abdomen and follow it as it rises and falls with each breath.

4. If your attention wanders, that's completely normal! When that happens, gently return your focus to your breath. If possible, let the return to your breath be as gentle as the breath itself—not judging, but kind.

Challenge: You might be inclined to control your breath in some way. When that happens, take a few deep breaths to reset the urge to control and return to a natural breath.

Broaden Your Comfort Zone

Time: 7 minutes

*"There are opportunities even in the
most difficult moments."*

—*Wangari Maathai*

Given that we can't control our lives or our surroundings,
the next best thing we can do is to learn how to find
ease—even in the midst of discomfort. Mindfulness helps
us do exactly that, not by turning *away* from discomfort
but by turning *toward* it. This doesn't mean we need to
throw ourselves into the deep end of discomfort before
we're ready; that would be an unwise use of the practice.
Instead, we can lean into it in a way that simultaneously
takes care of ourselves while also broadening our comfort zone.

Steps:

1. Settle into a pose and relax into a stillness that
    doesn't make you feel trapped or rigid. Take a
    few deep breaths to help you settle. Whenever
    you're ready, breathe naturally, whether that's
    through your mouth or nose.

2. As best you can, for the few minutes of this practice, stay still, knowing that the more still you remain, the more the everyday tension you carry will become apparent.

3. What are you feeling right now? What parts of your body are calling for your attention? What are the thoughts that accompany these sensations? Are you able to tune in to the body parts that are not tense or sensitive?

4. Notice any urge that may arise to shift positions to relieve any discomfort you may be feeling. This is a completely normal reaction; however, see if it's possible to be with the sensations for at least three more breaths before adjusting, if at all.

5. Once your meditation practice has ended, move in any way you like, trying to be present for the flood of relief you may feel from adjusting your posture.

Challenge: There's a fine line between discomfort and pain. If you suspect that the discomfort can cause injury, don't endure it—please adjust!

This Body Breathing

Time: 12 minutes

"Please know your immeasurable worth.
Every breath you take is exquisite."
—Unknown

Although this meditation is great on its own, it can be quite effective when things feel intense or overwhelming. Although a go-to mindfulness technique when feeling agitated is to tune in to the breath, if you're already breathing superficially, it can actually exacerbate the agitation. Instead, feeling where your breath moves your body, trying to notice the subtle and unexpected places, is an effective way to both ground the mind and widen the perspective, tending to your agitated heart and mind.

Steps:

1. Once you've settled into your posture, listen and tune in to your own breathing.

2. Where do you feel your breath the most? You may automatically place your attention on a particular part of the body, but for a few moments, pretend this is the first time you are

being asked to notice your breath. For these few moments, just receive your breath.

3. Wherever you feel your breath the most, be particularly mindful of it for 10 to 12 breaths.

4. Ask yourself and observe: How does your breath move your body? What are its qualities—smooth, choppy, long, short, cold, warm, light, heavy, floating, blocked, tingling? Are the sensations of your inhale stronger or more obvious than your exhale, or is it the reverse?

5. Expand your awareness to include your entire body and feel your breath as a full-body sensation, from head to toe. Instead of just one part of the body expanding and contracting with each breath, feel the whole body moving with it, even if the sensations are subtle.

Challenge: Our breath can sometimes "get shy," making it hard to feel. If that happens, turn your attention to another anchor that feels more easeful.

Let's Get Physical

Time: 12 minutes

"Our ideas are transformed sensations."

—*Étienne Bonnot de Condillac*

Although the body itself can't speak, it certainly communicates with us, and it does so through the realm of physical sensations. For example, sensations might be telling us that something is pleasant, like a movement or an emotion, or unpleasant, like a boundary being violated. Or sensations might be telling us that we need to pay attention to our surroundings. These "messages" can point to particular emotions we're feeling, even if we don't yet have the words to pinpoint what they are. Regardless of our experience, physical sensations are a portal to our mindfulness practice and a gateway to a rich, inner world.

Steps:

1. Take a comfortable position and begin to notice the sensations of the breath, feeling it move in and out of the body.

2. As you sit feeling the breath, you may notice that sensations arise in your body in a way

that is strong enough to take your attention away from your breath. The sensations may even become the dominant experience. If this is the case, try not to struggle to push away the sensations. Instead, use the sensations as your new point of focus.

3. Make a silent mental note of what you are experiencing right now: pain . . . tingling . . . itchiness . . . . Find a word that most resembles what you are feeling, but know that you don't need to find the "perfect" word.

4. Integrate the same quality of awareness as you did to note the breath—relaxed, spacious, open, not trying to control or change your experience.

5. Notice if the sensation is pleasant and notice the tendency to cling to it, to keep it. Notice if the sensation is unpleasant and any tendency to push it away. Relax and open again so you can be with whatever is there without grasping or pushing it away.

Coming Back to Your Senses

Time: 10 minutes

> *"Not the senses I have but what I do
> with them is my kingdom."*
> —Helen Keller

Although obvious, until I started meditating, I never actually realized that the way we take in the world around us is through our sense doors. On top of it, most often unbeknownst to us, we are constantly reacting to and strategizing in response to the things we hear, see, feel, smell, and taste. Given this and our human tendency to turn seemingly simple experiences into a whole set of reactions and strategies, having mindfulness at the door of each of our senses can help us discern which experiences are worth reacting to.

Steps:

1. Give yourself a few moments to simply observe any sounds, movements, or sensations in your field of awareness.

2. Turn your attention to your breath, and follow closely the in and out of six slow, deep breaths.

3. Begin to loosen your grip on the awareness of your breath. Imagine you're leaving one hand of attention on the breath, while your other hand explores the things happening right now that are attracting your attention. These can be sounds, sensations, smells, tastes, images (even if your eyes are closed), and thoughts.

4. When one of the senses distracts you, don't try to shut it out. Instead, let it in and acknowledge it by silently saying to yourself "hearing" or "feeling," for example. We are not trying to analyze what is happening by occupying ourselves with who, what, and why type questions, but rather we want to simply be aware of what is happening.

5. As soon as you're done acknowledging or noting whatever it is that caught your attention, return to your breath. Even if you have to bring your attention back over and over and over, that's the practice right now.

Adjustment: Refine your attention even further by noticing how the feeling, sound, sensation, or thought physically manifests in your body, mentally noting any specific sensations.

Sending Love

Time: 12 minutes

"We're all just walking each other home."

—Ram Dass

Having a hard time seeing someone you love suffer speaks volumes of the love and care you feel. Yet, for some, your version of "being compassionate" might be to jump into problem-solving mode and offer the sufferer a list of solutions and actions to help move them past their suffering. Although this comes from a wholesome place—wanting a person you love to be happy and filled with ease—this tendency often leaves a loved one not feeling seen or heard. To counter this, this particular mindfulness exercise will allow you to create space for what your loved one is going through or feeling, so they can feel supported exactly as they are.

Steps:

1. Begin in a position that is a reflection of kindness or compassion. Settle your awareness by noticing the sounds around you, the sensations in your body, or your breath.

2. Bring to mind a loved one who might be going through a difficult time. Take a moment to feel in your body your natural care for them.

3. Become aware of their suffering. If it feels appropriate, place your hands over your heart and wish them well, opening your heart to send them ease, to help them carry their pain and meet it with compassion.

4. Inwardly recite the phrases:

   May you be held in compassion.
   May you be free from pain and sorrow.
   May you be at peace.

5. Repeat these phrases over and over while holding them in your heart. Feel free to adjust the phrases in any way so they are more significant to you or your loved one.

Challenge: If bringing to mind a loved one's suffering leads you to feel overwhelmed, shift your focus to something more neutral, like your breath, or open your eyes.

Root Down, Reach Up

Time: 7 minutes

"Feeling is the secret."
—*Neville Goddard*

The Buddha taught that we can practice mindfulness in four poses: seated, standing, walking, and lying down. Some would say—and I happily agree—that there's even a fifth pose: everything in between! In other words, it's not the pose you're practicing in that matters but the quality of awareness that you bring to whatever it is you're doing. In this meditation, we are extending our mindfulness practice to include some stretching and movement, using the physical sensations that the movements bring as a doorway into our mindfulness practice.

Steps:

1. Stand with your feet hip-width apart. Soften your knees so that the weight of your body can be evenly distributed over both of your feet. Let your arms hang slightly away from the sides of your body and relax your shoulders and face.

2. Become aware of your surroundings—the temperature of the room, the lighting, sounds, and movements. Feel your entire body.

3. When the urge to move arises, reach up toward the sky or ceiling. Any amount of lift is perfect. There is no need to force beyond what feels good. If your neck allows, follow your hands, looking up between them.

4. As you reach toward the sky or ceiling, root your feet down. Does that help you reach higher? What sensations are present? Are the sensations pleasant, unpleasant, or neutral?

5. After a few breaths, bend your knees and fold at your hips, bending toward the ground. Relax your head and shoulders, letting all tension release toward the earth. What is your breath like right now?

6. When you're ready, keep your knees bent and unroll yourself, vertebra by vertebra. Try to feel each individual vertebra stack one on top of the next as you unroll.

7. Repeat as many times as you wish!

Adjustment: If you have high blood pressure, avoid folding down toward the ground. Instead, fold halfway, keeping your head above or level with your heart.

Stretch from Seat to Sky

Time: 12 minutes

"Be sincere; be brief; be seated."
—*Franklin D. Roosevelt*

Despite our best intentions, sometimes our meditation practice can remain a heady experience. This is caused by a few things, one being that we are using the mind to train the mind to calm down! Albeit an imperfect training, it's one that works, and so we carry on—with wisdom. During the times when we just can't seem to get out of our heads, bringing in some mindful movement to shift the energy and elicit sensation can serve as the perfect solution to drop our attention into the body.

Steps:

1. In a comfortable seated position, gently stack your head over your heart over your hips.

2. Take your time to arrive by breathing slowly and deeply for a minute or two, or about 12 breaths.

3. Reach your arms up to the sky or ceiling. Don't force in a way that might feel unpleasant. Hold this pose for a few breaths, inhaling fully into

your entire torso. Notice any sensations that have arisen with this movement.

4. Fold your body forward any amount, resting your arms and hands on the ground away from you. Take advantage of your exposed back and breathe deeply into your back body.

5. If thoughts arise about how you're "performing," let them float away by regrounding your attention into your body and its sensations.

6. Roll yourself up, stacking your vertebrae one on top of the next slowly, until you are back in your starting position.

7. Pause in this upright pose for another 12 breaths, feeling all the sensations that have been aroused from these simple, gentle movements.

8. Repeat these movements at least one more time. If you are sitting cross-legged, be sure to switch the leg that is in front with each repetition.

Relax Into Balance

Time: 5 minutes

"Balance is not something you find,
it's something you create."
—Jana Kingsford

A common expression is that we "lose balance," implying there was something to be lost in the first place. Although the feeling of balance may seem real, balance in and of itself is a mental construct that is dependent on many things. If we can remember to be mindful, it doesn't really matter if we're balanced or if we lost it. What matters is that our quality of kind attention remained.

Steps:

1. Stand on a solid surface with your feet together. Soften around your knees and relax your shoulders and arms. Take a few deep breaths.

2. Keeping your eyes open, fix a soft gaze on a point that doesn't move a few feet in front of you. Bring your attention to your feet and legs and notice any sensations present.

3. As you root your right foot down and lengthen all the way to the top of your head, lift your left heel.

4. Notice any sensations in your right ankle—wobbling or pulsing, for example. Embrace whatever sensations are present.

5. Lift your left foot to place the heel to the inside of your right ankle, your right calf, or your right inner thigh. Avoid placing the foot against the right knee.

6. Breathe naturally in this balance pose. If you like, bring your hands into prayer position in front of your chest or reach your arms to the sky or ceiling.

7. Lower your left foot and feel both feet, ankles, legs. Notice any urge to "shake it out." Resist the urge, and instead, stand mindfully. Feel balance returning on its own.

8. Whenever you're ready, repeat this on the other side.

Challenge: If you're feeling particularly wobbly, you can steady yourself by placing a hand on a wall or the back of a chair.

Neck Stretch

Time: 7 minutes

"The inspiration you seek is already within you. Be silent and listen."

—*Rumi*

Whether it's because of stress and anxiety or prolonged periods of looking down at our devices, more of us are finding ourselves with a tense neck and tense shoulders. If this tightness goes unattended, it can lead to reduced mobility and even headaches. Eventually, with sustained and consistent practice, mindfulness can act as a preventative tool. In addition to our becoming aware of our posture and managing our stress better, both of which positively impact our tense neck and shoulders, doing these simple movements with mindfulness can awaken these areas in a way that may not have been possible before.

Steps:

1. After you've settled into stillness, take a few deep breaths to help you arrive more fully to this moment.

2. Become aware of your neck and shoulders and any sensations that may be present in these areas. Can you name what you're feeling?

3. Drop your chin toward your chest and begin to roll your head from side to side, moving at a pace at which you can stay mindful. As you do this, notice the mix of pleasant, unpleasant, and neutral sensations.

4. The next time your right ear is over your right shoulder, pause there and breathe deeply. Reach your left shoulder down and away to intensify the stretch. Send your breath to the places where you feel tension or tightness.

5. After a few breaths there, bring your chin back to your chest and lift the head. Pause here for a few moments to simply feel. Be particularly curious about all the sensations present.

6. When you're ready, repeat these movements on the other side. Feel free to repeat the movements as many times as you like.

Challenge: As your ear is over your shoulder, reach your opposite hand down and away from you. You can even add a nod and shake of your head.

Massage Your
Way to Mindfulness

Time: 10 minutes

*"Self-care means giving yourself
permission to pause."*
—Cecilia Tran

Some days, it can be hard to feel the body and its sensations no matter how much we might try. The following meditation is one of my favorite ways to connect to the body because it doesn't take long—and it feels good! Some long-term benefits of this particular practice include a reduction of tension and stress, as well as an increase in one's emotional intelligence. Doing this regularly and tuning in to how something as simple as this practice can benefit you will begin to show you that self-care is not a luxury but a necessity.

Steps:

1. With soft wrists and fingers, gently tap your entire head and face. When you reach your eyes, instead of tapping, gently massage your eyelids in sweeping motions. Tap the front of your neck and throat, too.

2. Lower your hands and feel the energy and sensations present at the face, head, and neck.

3. Make a soft fist with your right hand by placing your thumb on the inside of your fingers. Outstretch your left arm, palm facing down, and gently thump the upper part of your arm. Make your way to your shoulder, lightly tapping the back of the neck. Travel back down the upper arm, turn your left palm up, and thump the inner arm and left side chest.

4. Take a moment to feel the left arm, shoulder, and chest, noticing any vibrations or tingling.

5. Repeat steps 3 and 4 on the right side, with your left hand in a soft fist.

6. With soft fingers, massage your belly area, sending kindness and compassion to this part of the body that is so often ignored.

7. Make soft fists with both your hands and lean forward. Gently massage your lower back.

8. Settle back into your meditation posture and feel the energy you've created running through your body.

Bring Life to Your Hike

Time: 15 minutes

**"Nature does not hurry,
yet everything is accomplished."**

—Lao Tzu

There are a few things that can immediately grab our attention in such a way that our mindfulness becomes undeniable. Being up close with animals, children (especially when they're not our own!), and nature make up part of those enthralling experiences. As a result, hiking with awareness can really enhance your time on the trail. Yet, if you bring to your hike a goal and hold to it tightly, that can be enough to prohibit not only mindfulness from being included but joy as well. For this practice, it is best to leave all objectives aside and practice being with each step.

Steps:

1. At the trailhead or park entrance, stop and take in your surroundings—feel the air around you, take in the smells and sights, and tune in to how your body feels.

2. Visualize the trail or path you plan to take. If it's a familiar route, bring to mind any

challenging parts so you can be particularly aware of them when you come across them. As you visualize yourself on your hike, try to include how you want to feel.

3. Start your hike or walk, and all throughout pay attention to your body, breath, and thoughts.

4. When a sight, smell, or sound catches your attention, come to standing and really take it in. Feel the impact this sight, smell, or sound has on your body.

5. When your mind wanders to things not on or about your hike, stop, take a deep breath to ground yourself, and continue on.

6. Pay attention for subtle internal reactions such as "This is hard" or "I've done enough; I'll turn back soon," which are rooted in initial impressions of pleasant, unpleasant, and neutral. Shift your focus from the thoughts to the feeling tone instead and notice if this changes your hike or endurance in any way.

Build a Backbone

Time: 10 minutes

*"We believe that it takes a strong back
and a soft front to face the world."*

—Joan Halifax

As beings that walk on two legs, with eyes positioned to see forward and minds conditioned to think ahead, we often forget about the back of our body. As a result, once we start practicing mindfulness, we don't realize we often focus on the front of our body when we tune in to our breath or look for physical sensations. This practice helps to balance this out and has two particular benefits: It helps to strengthen the muscles in our back and begins to enliven this area that we so often ignore.

Steps:

1. Spread out a yoga mat or blanket on a soft surface and lay face-down, resting your chin or forehead on the ground with your hands beneath your shoulders. Take a few deep breaths, sending your breath to the sides of your body and into your back.

2. Place your elbows on the ground in line with your shoulders and align your hands with your elbows, palms down to the ground. Your arms will be at a 90-degree angle. If you're able, slide your elbows forward so they are slightly higher than your shoulders.

3. Press the hands firmly down into the ground and engage a pulling action. Your hands won't move but they're pulling at the ground as if you are trying to pull yourself forward. As you do this, inhale and lift your chest and head off the ground any amount, paying particular attention to your lower back, making sure not to pinch it.

4. When you need to exhale, lower yourself down and rest on one ear. Pause here for a few moments to feel the residual sensations from this simple movement.

5. Repeat this as many times as you like, alternating the ear you rest on between lifts.

Adjustment: This can also be done at a wall. Changing your relationship to gravity in this way makes the practice a little easier.

Swiftly Sweep

Time: 12 minutes

*"Be happy in the moment, that's enough.
Each moment is all we need, not more."*
—Mother Teresa

There are plenty of things we do in our lives that are for our well-being—many of which we enjoy doing and some of which we don't. In the latter category for me is sweeping the floor. Much like my running practice, and sometimes even my meditation practice, I'm happiest not as I'm doing it but once it's done. Whatever it is for you, approaching it in much the same way as this practice turns sweeping into a meditation—by being present for the process and not overly focused on the outcome—may make it go by faster, and perhaps even make it enjoyable.

Steps:

1. Stand in the area you have to sweep with your broom in hand. Do a quick standing meditation. What do you notice about your body? What kinds of thoughts are passing through your mind? How do you feel about sweeping right now?

2. When you're ready, begin to sweep. For the first few minutes, sweep slowly, letting each stroke of the broom come to completion before putting the broom down to sweep again.

3. Pay attention to the movements of your body, the sounds of the broom, and what your eyes are looking at.

4. What feelings are present? Repulsion at dirt? Satisfaction at the collecting of the dirt? Any and all feelings are welcome here.

5. Continue at this pace for a few more sweeps. You can eventually quicken your pace, moving at a speed where you can remain mindful.

6. When you're at the end of the task and you're about to gather the dust in the dustpan, notice any judgments, thoughts, and sensations— about the dirt, cleaning tools, or the little specks of dirt that are hard to get into the dustpan.

7. Extend your practice to include throwing the dust and dirt into the bin.

Choosing Forgiveness

Time: 12 minutes

"It's one of the greatest gifts you can give yourself, to forgive. Forgive everybody."

—Maya Angelou

When bolstered by sayings like "forgive and forget," we might be quick to forgive someone without ever really tending to our own feelings of hurt, or we might let someone back into our life despite our better judgment. For these reasons, forgiveness is often the most challenging and misunderstood quality. It doesn't condone the past, it doesn't mean we need to stay connected to anyone who has caused us pain, nor is it weak or naive. Forgiveness takes time and is really about not leaving anyone out of your heart, including yourself, for any hurt that may have been caused.

Steps:

1. Begin in a position that is an expression of kindness. If it feels appropriate, place your hands over your heart and tune in to your body.

2. Bring to mind anyone you may have harmed. Hold them lightly in your awareness, and silently say, "For any way that I have caused

you harm, knowingly or unknowingly,
in thought, word, or deed, I ask for your
forgiveness."

3. Pause for a few moments, letting these words
land in your body and heart.

4. In much the same way, bring to mind anyone
who might have hurt or harmed you. Silently
say, "For any way that you have caused me
harm, knowingly or unknowingly, in thought,
word, or deed, may I forgive you," leaving a
long pause after reciting the phrase.

5. Next, for yourself, silently say, "For any way
that I have caused harm to myself, through
judgment, action, self-blame, indifference,
knowingly or unknowingly, in thought, word,
or deed, may I forgive myself. And if I cannot
do so in this moment, may I be able to forgive
myself in the future."

6. Let any feelings arise with this phrase, holding
yourself in kindness.

From Painful to Mindful

Time: 12 minutes

"The cure for the pain is in the pain."

—*Rumi*

A natural human tendency is to want to avoid anything unpleasant, and even more so anything painful. Like so many of the meditations we've explored together so far, the most immediate way in which we can find any sort of freedom is not by avoiding pain but by moving toward it. However, jumping into feeling the pain before you're ready could alter your relationship to what you're feeling, and not for the better. As a result, this meditation invites you to gently start leaning into it so that you can eventually establish a new relationship to your pain.

Steps:

1. Bring your attention to the sounds happening around you—inside the room, outside the room, close to you, far from you. Practice being with them just as they are, not naming them or wondering where they're coming from.

2. Turn your attention to a part of your body that is not hurting at the moment. Notice any

sensations in that area, however subtle the sensations or small the area.

3. Become aware of a part of your body that is in pain right now. Even if for a very brief moment, try to turn your attention toward it, and then shift your awareness back to the sounds going on around you.

4. Check in with what it was like turning toward the pain or discomfort, sensing into what you were able to feel. This is not to be underestimated! You are already on your way to developing a new and healing relationship with your pain, as well as your mind and body.

5. If you found it challenging, that is completely normal. The good news is this is a skill that can be cultivated with patience and kindness. Whenever you feel ready, return to steps 3 and 4; otherwise, continue following the sounds around you.

Peace of Food

Time: 12 minutes

"We're all under the same sky and walk the same earth; we're alive together during the same moment."
—*Maxine Hong Kingston*

Mindfulness is so all-encompassing that we can integrate it into anything we do, allowing us to never be too far from our practice. Even if you don't have the time or space to practice regularly for extended periods of time, you will begin to see that there are countless opportunities throughout the day during which you can be mindful. With this practice, you'll discover how to eat mindfully, which suddenly grants you at least three opportunities daily to practice. For this meditation, it's best to have some food in front of you, whether it's a whole meal or a snack.

Steps:

1. Once you have served yourself some food, pause and take a deep breath.

2. With your eyes open, take in the different shapes, textures, and colors of your food. Give a silent thanks to everyone who has helped make eating this food possible: the server

or cashier who sold you the food, anyone involved in preparing it, the staff where you bought the food, the delivery people who helped bring the food from the farm to your grocery store or restaurant, the farmers—those who planted, nurtured, and harvested the ingredients—even the sun, wind, water, and earth.

3. Figure out what you'll eat first and become aware of your body. Is your mouth watering or are you tense anywhere? Notice whatever sensations may be present.

4. Hold your utensils and take a moment to feel them. Pick up some food and feel your arm lift your food toward your mouth.

5. Open your mouth and put the food in. Before chewing, become aware of what immediately grabs your attention. Notice any tastes, smells, sounds, textures, or physical reactions. Begin to chew slowly, eventually swallowing. Notice any sense of enjoyment and how that enjoyment may ebb and flow as you get sated.

CONTINUED

6. Continue eating in this way, perhaps at a slightly quicker pace without losing your quality of attention.

Adjustment: Try this the next time you share a meal with others. Make it accessible by just focusing on eating a few bites mindfully.

Stand by Your Suffering

Time: 15 minutes

*"Although the world is full of suffering, it is
also full of the overcoming of it."*
—Helen Keller

We are so adept at avoiding that which we don't want to
feel or experience that we spend a lot of our time running away from perceived or future pain. At the touch of
unpleasantness, the mind can jump into storytelling about
what the pain means and how it can affect our future. As a
result, past pains begin to dictate our future—we decide
prematurely that we will feel pain before we actually feel
it. Although in many circumstances that might be true,
we can never be sure how our body will show up at any
given moment.

Steps:

1. Bring your attention to the sounds happen-
    ing around you—inside the room, outside the
    room, close to you, far from you. Practice being
    with them just as they are, not naming them or
    wondering where they're coming from.

CONTINUED

2. Bring a light touch of mindfulness to the parts of your body that are in pain. You don't need to spend much time at all sensing into your pain, just as much as you can bear, however brief.

3. Acknowledge and honor the part of you that doesn't want to be in pain. The deep desire to be pain-free is coming from a wholesome place—wishing for yourself less suffering in this world. Hold this part of you with tenderness and kindness.

4. Inwardly recite these phrases:

   May I be held in compassion.
   May I be free from pain and sorrow.
   May I be at peace.

5. Let any feelings arise with the words, even if they seem contradictory. If need be, adjust the phrases so that you find ones that best open you.

6. After repeating the phrases over and over for a few minutes, come back to the sounds going on around you.

Late Day Reset

Time: 7 minutes

*"Every action has an impact, choose wisely
the impact you want to have."*
—Mindy Hall

Although you might have started your day with sincere
and good intentions, distractions, busy-ness, or simple
forgetfulness tend to get the better of us. This practice is
designed to help you recommit to your original intentions
and is best done later in the day, like the late afternoon or
early evening. Try it when you've changed environments,
like arriving home from work or school, or you've changed
situations, like going from being with co-workers to being
with family. It can serve as a way to reset and leave whatever happened in the first part of your day in the past.

Steps:

1. Settle into a position of ease and tune in to the
   parts of your body touching the ground. Take
   a few deep breaths to help you arrive more
   fully at this moment.

2. Working your way backward, visualize the ear-
   lier part of your day—what you were just doing,

CONTINUED

where, and with whom, your afternoon, lunch, and morning. What were some of the things you did? Who did you come across, if anyone? How did you feel? Picture your breakfast or morning beverages, if you had any, and even remember how and when you woke up. Try to imagine your day with as much detail as you can.

3. Once again, tune in to the parts of your body touching the ground or your breath.

4. Now bring to mind the rest of your day—how you'll be spending your time and with whom. Visualize how you'd like to be for the rest of your day—patient, kind, or relaxed, for example. You may or may not be able to be the way you'd like, but you're setting the intention for this quality to arise more easily.

5. One last time, feel your body touching the ground. Take a deep breath and exhale.

360° Breath

Time: 15 minutes

"Focus on the miracle that your breath is."
—Jacqueline Whitney

To me, the practice of mindfulness is one of coming home—to our body and ourselves. We do this by gradually growing increasingly aware of all the parts of ourselves that make us who we are, internally and externally, instead of continuing to focus solely on the parts that we see most often or feel most obviously. The following meditation invites you to pay attention to an often overlooked area— the back body—and how it moves with each breath, adding to your full-body awareness.

Steps:

1. Be able to breathe with ease in your meditation posture. Take a few deep breaths to create space in the body and mind.

2. Bring your hands to your chest or abdomen. Feel the temperature of your hands, the contact with your body, and any other sensations.

CONTINUED

3. For 12 slow, deep breaths, feel your hands rise and fall with each inhale and exhale.

4. Move your hands to the sides of your rib cage by either crossing your arms in front of you or, if your shoulders allow, widening your elbows and resting your hands on your sides. Tune in to any sensations, pleasant or unpleasant, of this arm placement.

5. With your hands, feel your rib cage expand and contract for 12 slow, deep breaths.

6. Lower your hands. Bring your attention to your back, particularly the kidney area, which is at the base of your back ribs. Sense how your breath moves this part of your body, again for 12 breaths.

7. For the rest of the meditation, continue with your slow, deep breaths, feeling your body expand and contract in all four directions (front, back, right side, and left side).

Your Inner Breath

Time: 15 minutes

*"Listen, are you breathing just a little,
and calling it a life?"*
—Mary Oliver

When being mindful of the breath, we can get so concentrated on a certain quality or focused on a part of the body, we may not feel the breath as a full-body experience. In addition to food, water, and sunshine, the breath is a vital way in which we get fed and energized, yet we may be aware of it in only a broad way. This meditation invites you to attune more deeply to your breath and body, sensing how energy gets sent to your entire body with each inhale, and how each exhale cleanses your entire body.

Steps:

1. Spend a few minutes quieting your mind by gathering your attention around your breath. Begin by noticing the more obvious movements of the body in relation to your breath, like the chest, abdomen, or back body.

2. Get even more curious about the qualities of your breath. How is it moving in and out of

CONTINUED

your body? What parts rise and fall, expand and contract?

3. Eventually, turn your attention to the even more subtle movements of your breath, observing if one side of the body moves more freely than the other, or if the body doesn't expand fully in some areas with each inhale.

4. Finally, for the remainder of the practice, when you inhale, tune in to how breathing in sends energy to your entire body, all the way to the tips of your fingers and toes. When it's time to exhale, sense how exhaling draws out old or stagnant energy from all the parts of your body.

Count Your Way to Sleep

Time: 15 minutes

*"Dwell on the beauty of life. Watch the stars,
and see yourself running with them."*
—Marcus Aurelius

Some people treat sleep the same way they do their goals: If it's not happening, they try harder! That approach, though, is the very thing that prohibits them from falling asleep. This meditation soothes the busy mind by giving it the task of counting while simultaneously feeling each breath relax the body. A word of caution to goal-oriented folks: It's important to not get fixated on the numbers. Counting your exhales is a mundane task that won't grip or energize your mind, while it also keeps at bay the very thoughts that keep you awake.

Steps:

1. Tuck yourself into bed and take a few deep breaths. Lay on your back or side and do your best to stay still, since movement can energize the mind and bring energy to the body.

2. Breathe naturally and tune in to your breath, feeling your inhale and exhale. If you're

CONTINUED

laying on your back, place your hands on your abdomen or chest and feel them rise and fall as your body expands and contracts with each breath.

3. Relax your eyebrows, eyes, and jaw. Release your shoulders and any other place you may be tensing.

4. Begin to calm your mind and body even further by counting your exhales. Silently say to yourself, "Inhaling . . . one . . . Inhaling . . . two . . . Inhaling . . . three . . . ." Keep the "volume" of your mental noting low, focusing your attention primarily on the sensations of your breath and on the numbers.

5. Your attention may drift. Don't worry if your mind wanders, just return your focus to your breathing.

6. In a relaxed way, see if you can get to 10. If you lose count, simply start again at one. Once you get to 10, count back down to one. Getting to 10 or one is not really important; keeping a relaxed effort is what's key.

A Final Word

A good and lasting meditation practice doesn't end when the timer goes off. The most telling place where the quality of our practice speaks is in the way we live our lives, not in how calm, quiet, or pleasant the mind may be.

Mindfulness is an invitation to wake up to the new and exciting, as well as the familiar and mundane, in equal measures. For example, the capacity to breathe and to read this book are gifts that we tend to forget when we're wrapped up in our own world. Yet when we practice mindfulness, we can remember that being able to breathe or to see and read is indeed precious, and we don't need to wait for something to threaten to take away these capacities to remind us of their brilliance.

This precious human life is made up of precious human days and precious human moments. How we spend them is important—how we spend our time, how we live together, and most importantly, how we treat ourselves and each other. Mindfulness teaches us that what we do doesn't matter as much as how we do it. The invitation then becomes to do things with openness, kindness, and compassion. We don't have to be born open, kind, and compassionate; this practice slowly teaches us how to cultivate these qualities.

This book was written with the intention that your practice begins here but doesn't end here. I sincerely hope your interest has been piqued and you are inclined to continue practicing and to explore the teachings of mindfulness more profoundly. If you're not sure how or where to dive deeper, check out the resources section for a list of ways your practice can be continue to be supported.

> *May your days be full of blessings.*
> *May you taste freedom from life's suffering.*
> *May you know deep peace.*

Resources

BOOKS

Awakening Through Love: Unveiling Your Deepest Goodness by John Makransky
This book offers an alternative way to practice loving-kindness meditation. Caretakers, social workers, nurses, and doctors find refuge in this approach, yet it is accessible to all.

Awakening Together: The Spiritual Practice of Inclusivity and Community by Larry Yang
This is one of my favorite books! Beautifully written, it explores the intersection of the internal work of meditation and the external work of bringing it into the world.

Dipa Ma: The Life and Legacy of a Buddhist Master by Amy Schmidt
Dipa Ma was an extremely influential presence within modern Buddhism, especially for women within it, who dedicated herself fully to practice after experiencing immense grief. In this biography of the Buddhist master,

you'll discover an incredibly loving side to what cansometimes feel like a dry or serious practice.

A Path With Heart: A Guide Through the Perils and Promises of Spiritual Life by Jack Kornfield
One of the first meditation books I read and the one I recommend to people the most. Jack Kornfield magically weaves storytelling with teachings and includes meditations at the end of almost every chapter.

The Revolutionary Art of Happiness: Loving-Kindness Meditation by Sharon Salzberg
This book is the go-to book for those who are looking to learn all about the heart practices of loving-kindness, compassion, sympathetic joy, and equanimity.

Time to Stand Up: An Engaged Buddhist Manifesto for Our Earth by Thanissara
This is a very necessary book for our current times. It retells the story of the Buddha, a great activist of his time, and links it to the climate urgency that our earth is facing.

The Way of Tenderness: Awakening Through Race, Sexuality, and Gender by Zenju Earthlyn Manuel
Here's another one of my favorites. It explores the complex intersection of practice with identity.

ORGANIZATIONS/NETWORKS

Buddhist Insight Network: If you are interested in finding a group with whom you can practice in person, this site offers a comprehensive directory.

BuddhistInsightNetwork.org

Inward Bound Mindfulness Education: A nonprofit organization that organizes and hosts mindfulness retreats for teenagers in the United States, Canada, and the United Kingdom.

IBME.info

Kalyana Mitta: This means spiritual friendship and, specifically in our context, a network of spiritual friends you travel with on this path. In the link below, you'll find instructions on creating your own group of spiritual friends if you can't find a group of people to practice with.

SpiritRock.org/kalyana-mitta-guidelines

Spirit Rock Meditation Center: This renowned meditation retreat center based in California offers a beautiful setting with skilled teachers if you're interested in intensive meditation practice. (I teach here!)

SpiritRock.org

True North Insight: A nonprofit organization based in Eastern Canada that offers intensive meditation retreats, weekly classes, day-long classes, study programs, and more. I'm a teacher with this organization and am also on the board.

TrueNorthInsight.org

MEDITATION APPS

These apps take the accessibility of meditation practice to whole new levels. Although in-person practice with a group or contact with a teacher is recommended when possible, apps can help maintain and sustain a personal practice.

Below are a few apps to which I'm a contributor:

Insight Timer: The largest free online meditation community and library of guided meditations with contributing teachers from all over the world.

InsightTimer.com

Liberate App: A meditation app that has the core values of equality and inclusivity. It was created by people of color and features teachers of color.

LiberateMeditation.com

Meditation Studio App: I'm humbled to accompany over 60 other qualified meditation teachers on this app. **MeditationStudioApp.com**

Neo Travel Your Mind: A truly original app! It is designed to take you on a journey, and with the high-quality soundscapes and catered meditations, you will feel both out of this world and into your body. **NeoMeditation.com/en**

HOW TO SIT

If you would like visual examples with more detailed instructions on the different ways in which you can set yourself up to sit for practice, check out this PDF I created.

DawnMauricio.com/shop/howtosit

References

Alidina, Shamash. "Nine Ways Mindfulness Reduces Stress." *Mindful.* July 17, 2019. http://www.Mindful .org/9-ways-mindfulness-reduces-stress.

Baer, Ruth A. "Mindfulness Training as a Clinical Intervention: A Conceptual and Empirical Review." *Clinical Psychology: Science and Practice* 10, no. 1 (May 2006): 125–43. doi: 10.1093/clipsy/bpg015.

Berman, Marc G., John Jonides, and Richard L. Lewis. "In Search of Decay in Verbal Short-Term Memory." *Journal of Experimental Psychology, Learning, Memory and Cognition* 35, no. 2 (March 2009): 317–33. doi: 10.1037/a0014873.

Black, David S., Gillian A. O'Reilly, Richard Olmstead, Elizabeth C. Breen, and Michael R. Irwin. "Mindfulness Meditation and Improvement in Sleep Quality and Daytime Impairment Among Older Adults with Sleep Disturbances: A Randomized Clinical Trial." *JAMA Internal Medicine* 175, no. 4 (April 2015): 494–501. doi: 10.1001/ jamainternmed.2014.8081.

Bowen, Sarah, Neha Chawla, and G. Alan Marlatt. *Mindfulness-Based Relapse Prevention for Addictive*

Behaviors: A Clinician's Guide. New York, NY: The Guilford Press, 2011.

Clarke, Tainya C., Patricia M. Barnes, Lindsey I. Black, Barbara J. Stussman, and Richard L. Nahin. "Use of Yoga, Meditation, and Chiropractors Among U.S. Adults Aged 18 and Over." *National Center for Health Statistics,* Data Brief no. 325 (November 2018): 1–8. http://www.CDC.gov/nchs/data/databriefs/db325-h.pdf.

Goyal, Mayank, S. Singh, E. M. Sibinha, N. F. Gould, A. Rowland-Seymour, R. Sharma, Z. Berger et al. "Meditation Programs for Psychological Stress and Well-Being: A Systematic Review and Meta-analysis." *JAMA Internal Medicine* 174, no. 3 (March 2017): 357–68. doi: 10.1001/jamainternmed.2013.13018.

Greenberg, J., V. L. Romero, S. Elkin-Frankston, M. A. Bezdek, E. H. Schumacher, and S. W. Lazar. "Reduced Interference in Working Memory Following Mindfulness Training Is Associated with Increases in Hippocampal Volume." *Brain Imaging and Behavior* 13, no. 2 (April 2019): 366–76. doi: 10.1007/s11682-018-9858-4.

Hölzel, Britta K., James Carmody, Mark Vangel, Christina Congleton, Sita M. Yerramsetti, Tim Gard, and Sara W. Lazar. "Mindfulness Practice

Leads to Increases in Regional Brain Gray Matter Density." *Psychiatry Research: Neuroimaging* 191, no. 1 (January 2011): 36–43. doi: 10.1016/j.pscychresns.2010.08.006.

Karelaia, Natalia. "Why Mindful Individuals Make Better Decisions." *INSEAD Knowledge.* July 23, 2014. https://Knowledge.INSEAD.edu/leadership-management/why-mindful-individuals-make-better-decisions-3479.

Lazar, Sara W., Catherine E. Kerr, Rachel H. Wasserman, Jeremy R. Gray, Douglas N. Greve, Michael T. Treadway, Metta McGarvey et al. "Meditation Experience Is Associated with Increased Cortical Thickness." *Neuroreport* 16, no. 17 (November 2005): 1893–97. doi: 10.1097/01.wnr.0000186598.66243.19.

Loucks, Eric B., William R. Nardi, Roee Gutman, Ian M. Kronish, Frances B. Saadeh, Yu Li, Anna E. Wentz et al. "Mindfulness-Based Blood Pressure Reduction (MB-BP): Stage 1 Single-Arm Clinical Trial." *PLOS One* 14, no. 11 (November 2019): e0223095. doi: 10.1371/journal.pone.0223095.

Lu, Stacy. "Mindfulness and Mood Disorders in the Brain." *Monitor on Psychology* 46, no. 3 (March 2015): 50. http://www.APA.org/monitor/2015/03/mindfulness-mood.

Powell, Alvin. "When Science Meets Mindfulness." *Harvard Gazette*. April 9, 2018. http://News.Harvard.edu/gazette/story/2018/04/harvard-researchers-study-how-mindfulness-may-change-the-brain-in-depressed-patients.

Prebish, Charles. *Buddhism: The American Experience*. Journal of Buddhist Ethics Online Books, 2004.

Sancho, Marta, Marta de Gracia, Rita C. Rodriguez, Núria Mallorquí-Bagué, Jéssica Sánchez-González, Joan Trujols, Isabel Sánchez, Susana Jiménez-Murcia, and Jose M. Menchón. "Mindfulness-Based Interventions for the Treatment of Substance and Behavioral Addictions: A Systematic Review." *Frontiers in Psychiatry*, March 29, 2018. doi: 10.3389/fpsyt.2018.00095.

Schulte, Brigid. "Harvard Neuroscientist: Meditation Not Only Reduces Stress, Here's How It Changes Your Brain." *Washington Post*. May 26, 2015. http://www.WashingtonPost.com/news/inspired life/wp/2015/05/26/harvard-neuroscientist-meditation-not-only-reduces-stress-it-literally-changes-your-brain.

Trousselard, M., D. Steiler, D. Claverie, and F. Canini. "The History of Mindfulness Put to the Test of Current Scientific Data: Unresolved Questions." *Encephale-Revue de Psychiatrie Clinique*

Biologique et Therapeutique 40, no. 6 (December
2014): 474–80. doi: 10.1016/j.encep.2014.08.006.
Turner, Beth M., Sergio Paradiso, Cherie L. Marvel,
Ronald Pierson, Laura L. Boles Ponto, Richard D.
Hichwa, and Robert G. Robinson. "The Cerebellum
and Emotional Experience." *Neuropsychologica*
45, no. 6 (March 2007): 1331–41. doi: 10.1016/j
.neuropsychologia.2006.09.023.
University of Minnesota. "Mindfulness for Physical Pain."
Accessed December 19, 2019. http://www.Taking
Charge.csh.umn.edu/mindfulness-physical-pain.

Index

ACKNOWLEDGMENTS

I would like to thank and acknowledge the following people, because without them, I would not be the person or the teacher I am today.

To the city of Montreal, the only place I've called home. Thank you for your consistent support and encouragement and for being open to my teachings since day one, no matter how clumsy they sometimes were. It is because of the safe ground you provided that I was able to grow and evolve so much.

To my mama, Della, and my "second mom," Auntie Ellen. There will never be enough expressions of gratitude for the ways you're present in my life, for being part of my first sangha, and for being my first examples of strength and resilience.

Thank you, Dana, my therapist extraordinaire, for both lifting me up and keeping me grounded in your gentle and unassuming ways.

Gullu, my Dharma husband! Thank you for your eyes and generosity, and for sharing your wisdom.

To True North Insight, my first spiritual home. Thank you for giving me a place to grow from a shy volunteer to a teacher and board member. I look forward to all the ways we'll continue to grow together.

To Spirit Rock Meditation Center, for catapulting my practice and teaching in ways I only dreamed of.

To my love, François. Thank you for being my number one cheerleader. With you, anything and everything feels possible, no matter how messy I may get in my process.

Pascal, there are no words for the impact you've had in my life. You are so much to me—teacher, friend, and steady presence in my life. Thank you for seeing me in ways I don't always see myself, and for reflecting what you see back to me.

ABOUT THE AUTHOR

 **Dawn Mauricio** has been practicing and studying Vipassanā Meditation since 2005, regularly sitting long intensive meditation retreats in Canada, the United States, Thailand, Myanmar, and South Africa. She is a meditation retreat teacher for True North Insight and Spirit Rock Meditation Center and for teenagers with Inward Bound Mindfulness Education. Dawn is a value- and purpose-oriented teacher with a passion for inclusivity and is known to teach with a playful, dynamic, accessible, and heartfelt approach. You can find her teaching intensive meditation retreats, day-long retreats, and mindfulness workshops in Canada, the United States, and online at DawnMauricio.com.

Printed in the USA
CPSIA information can be obtained
at www.ICGtesting.com
CBHW081058120224
R14898600001B/R148986PG4145CBX00011B9

9 781646 116676